social sweets
Jason Atherton

social sweets

Jason Atherton

Absolute Press
An imprint of Bloomsbury Publishing Plc

50 Bedford Square   1385 Broadway
London   New York
WC1B 3DP   NY 10018
UK   USA

www.bloomsbury.com

ABSOLUTE PRESS and the A. logo are trademarks of Bloomsbury Publishing Plc

First published 2015

British Library Cataloguing-in-Publication Data
A catalogue record for this book is available from the British Library.

Library of Congress Cataloguing-in-Publication data has been applied for.

ISBN: HB: 978-1-4729-0556-7
ePDF: 978-1-4729-2080-5
ePub: 978-1-4729-2079-9

2 4 6 8 10 9 7 5 3 1

Printed and bound in China by C&C Offset

To find out more about our authors and books visit www.bloomsbury.com. Here you will find extracts, author
interviews, details of forthcoming events and the option to sign up for our newsletters.

CONTENTS

DEDICATION

I dedicate this book to a person who has given up her whole life to live with me in a foreign land, away from her family and friends and all that she once knew as normality. Not only has she stood by me in life but also in love and most of all as my best friend. She has supported my life in food. As all chef widows out there know, it's not easy doing this, but my wife understands that my passion for food is the very thing that keeps the blood flowing through my veins. Irha, this book is for you. I love you so much. xxxx

INTRODUCTION

INTRODUCTION

When I embarked on my career in cooking many years ago, I always wanted to do the macho things like cooking the meat and fish, making the sauces and prepping the big boxes of fresh-picked wild mushrooms straight from the New Forest.

Then one day, when I was working at Chez Nico, our head chef Paul Flynn told me we were really short in the pastry section and that he wanted me to start working there straight away. At the time I didn't have much experience in this department and it seemed to be a specialist area. Well, that's what I had always assumed. So the next day, with some trepidation, I turned up at the pastry section and entered an amazing world of precise measurement and exact skill. There was no room for macho muscle-flexing there, just total concentration and, above all else, disciplined teamwork. I loved my time as a pastry chef so much that I promised myself I would become expert in all areas of the pastry section, from bread-making, baking and tarts to ice creams and sorbets, parfaits and bombes.

I want to share with you some of my favourite recipes for sweet dishes so that you can try them at home. With pastry work you can have a lot of fun while you are mastering the skills that will give you great satisfaction and pride. I still remember when I pulled my first loaf of bread out of the oven. It felt such a big deal. I hope you get the same pleasures from this book as I did learning, cooking and writing.

Best, Jason
London 2015

BREADS & MUFFINS

BREADS
& MUFFINS

24/ BRIOCHE LOAF 27/ FOUGASSE 28/ SOURDOUGH
31/ PAIN D'ÉPICES 33/ CHOCOLATE CHIP MUFFINS 34/ CORNBREAD MUFFINS

BAGUETTE

In France, bakeries churn out warm baguettes fresh from the oven throughout the day because these breads are best eaten within a couple of hours of baking. In the UK, we rarely have this luxury so all the more reason to try and make them yourself. The sense of accomplishment that you get from making your own baguettes is hard to beat. I recommend a long proving time as it helps to develop the flavour of the bread.

MAKES 2 LOAVES

815g strong white bread flour, plus
    extra for dusting
1 tablespoon fine sea salt
610ml tepid water
flavourless oil for brushing
12g fast-action dried yeast

Sift the flour and salt into the bowl of an electric mixer fitted with the dough hook. Make a well in the centre and pour in the water. Mix on low speed for a minute or so to combine the ingredients into an uneven mass. Cover the bowl with lightly oiled cling film and leave to rest for an hour.

Uncover the bowl and add the yeast to the dough. With the mixer on low speed, mix and knead the dough for about 10 minutes or until it is smooth and springy. Cover again with the oiled cling film and leave to prove for 30 minutes.

Now give the dough a couple of folds. Cover the bowl again and leave in the fridge overnight. (This slow proving time is crucial for developing the flavour of the baguette.)

The next day, divide the dough in half and shape each piece into a long baguette. To do this, flatten the piece of dough with the palm of your hand into a round shape, then take one side and fold it into the centre. Do the same on the opposite side. Then fold over in half so the two original folded edges meet. Press down to seal the seams together. Turn the dough seam side down and, pressing evenly with the palms of both hands, gently roll the dough backwards and forwards until you have stretched it to a baguette shape 30–35cm long. If the dough springs back as you roll it, allow it to rest for 5 minutes before continuing. For even baking, make sure the baguette shape is of a similar thickness throughout.

Place the baguettes on a floured baking sheet (or a floured baguette tray if you have one) and cover lightly with oiled cling film. Leave to rise in a warm place for about an hour or until doubled in size.

Preheat the oven to 220°C/Fan 200°C/Gas Mark 7. Dust the baguettes with flour, then slash the tops with a sharp knife. Place the baking sheet in the hot oven and give the oven walls a few sprays of water. Bake for about 20 minutes or until the baguettes are golden brown and crisp, and they sound hollow when tapped on the underside. Remove to a wire rack to cool. Best enjoyed freshly baked.

BREADS & MUFFINS

BASIC WHITE BREAD

If you have never made bread before, there is no better place to start than with a simple white loaf. This bread is ideal for making sandwiches or simply eaten freshly toasted with a slab of good butter. Once you've mastered making this, you can begin to customise the recipe to your liking. For wholemeal bread, replace half of the flour with strong wholemeal flour. I also like to add a mixture of flaxseeds, linseeds, poppy seeds and sesame seeds to make a beautiful seeded loaf.

MAKES 1 LARGE LOAF

450g strong white bread flour, plus
    extra for dusting
1 teaspoon fine sea salt
1½ teaspoons caster sugar
7g sachet fast-action dried yeast (or
    10g fresh yeast)
285–300ml cold water
flavourless oil for greasing

Combine the flour, salt, sugar and dried yeast in the bowl of an electric mixer fitted with the dough hook. (If using fresh yeast, start by putting it in a small bowl with the sugar, stirring in a little tepid water until creamy and leaving for a few minutes until the yeast activates and begins to froth.) Make a well in the centre of the flour mixture and pour in 285ml of the water (if using fresh yeast, pour the frothy mixture into the flour with the water). Mix on low speed until the ingredients come together to make a soft but not too sticky dough. If the dough seems too wet, add a little more flour; if it is too dry, add a little more water.

When the dough has come together and pulls away from the sides of the bowl, increase the mixer speed to medium and knead for about 5 minutes or until the dough is smooth. Transfer the dough to a lightly oiled bowl and cover it with an oiled piece of cling film. Leave to rise in a warm spot for 1–2 hours or until doubled in size.

Knock back the dough by gently punching it down, then lightly knead a few times. Shape it into a neat log and place in a greased 900g loaf tin. Cover with the oiled cling film and leave to rise for 1–2 hours or until the dough has once again doubled in size: an indentation should be left when you gently prod the dough with your finger.

Preheat the oven to 220°C/Fan 200°C/Gas Mark 7. Dust the risen loaf with a little flour, then slash the top with a sharp knife or clean razor blade. Bake for 30–35 minutes or until golden brown. Leave to cool for a few minutes, then turn out the loaf on to a wire rack and leave to cool completely. Store in a bread bin for up to 3 days or slice, wrap and freeze for a month.

MILK ROLLS

You can serve these soft buns warmed up as lovely dinner rolls but my kids adore them slathered with softened butter and strawberry jam for breakfast. Stuffed with slices of ham, cheese and cucumber, they are also good for the children's lunchbox.

MAKES 8 ROLLS

500g strong white bread flour, plus
    extra for dusting
14g dried yeast (or 2 x 7g sachets fast-
    action dried yeast)
15g milk powder
60g caster sugar
2 teaspoons fine sea salt
150ml water
50ml whole milk
2 medium eggs
75g unsalted butter, softened
flavourless oil for greasing
1 large egg yolk beaten with
    1 tablespoon water, for glazing

Mix together the flour, yeast, milk powder, sugar and salt in the bowl of an electric mixer fitted with the dough hook. Make a well in the centre. In a measuring jug, lightly beat together the water, milk and eggs. Pour this into the well. With the machine on low speed, mix until the ingredients come together into a dough. Gradually add the butter, mixing until incorporated. (If you find the mixture too sticky, add a little more flour; the dough should be soft and moist.)

Increase the mixer speed to medium and knead the dough for about 5 minutes or until it is smooth, shiny and elastic. Cover the bowl with a lightly greased piece of cling film and leave to rise in a warm spot until the dough has doubled in size.

Knock back the risen dough by punching it down, then lightly knead it on a lightly floured work surface. Divide the dough into eight pieces, each weighing about 120g, and shape each one into a neat ball. Arrange the balls, spaced well apart, on a lightly greased baking sheet. Cover with a lightly greased sheet of cling film and leave to rise in a warm place for 1–2 hours or until the dough balls have doubled in size: when lightly pressed with a finger, a slight indentation should be left.

Preheat the oven to 200°C/Fan 180°C/Gas Mark 6. Lightly brush the rolls with the egg yolk glaze, then bake for 15–20 minutes or until golden brown. Leave the rolls to cool for 5 minutes before transferring to a wire rack to cool completely. The rolls are best enjoyed freshly baked, but you can freeze them or keep them in a bread tin for a couple of days.

POTATO BREAD

This is a super moist loaf with a tender crumb and it makes good use of leftover mashed potatoes if you have any to hand. It is great for sandwiches and will keep well for about a week. For smoked salmon sandwiches, I sometimes add a teaspoonful of dried dill or caraways seeds to the dough during kneading.

MAKES 2 LOAVES

375g potatoes, such as Maris Piper
sea salt
50ml olive oil, plus extra for brushing
200g plain flour, plus extra for
    dusting
100g wholemeal flour
5g caster sugar
7g fast-action dried yeast

Peel the potatoes and cut into large chunks. Place exactly 300g into a large pan. Cover the potatoes with cold water, add a generous pinch of sea salt and bring to the boil. Reduce the heat slightly and cook the potatoes for 15–20 minutes or until they are soft but not falling apart. To test, pierce the thickest part of a chunk with a small knife – there should be no resistance.

Drain the potatoes in a colander set over a large bowl; reserve the cooking liquid. Return the potatoes to the hot pan and toss over a very low heat for 2–3 minutes or until any excess liquid has evaporated.

Finely mash the potatoes using a potato ricer. (Alternatively, push the potatoes through a fine sieve to get a very smooth mash.) Add the oil and mix well. Leave to cool.

Put all the remaining ingredients, including 1 teaspoon of sea salt, into the bowl of an electric mixer fitted with the dough hook. Give the mixture a stir and make a well in the middle, then add the mashed potatoes. Measure out 100ml of the potato cooking liquid and add this to the well too. Mix on low speed until a soft dough is formed. If it appears to be a little dry, add a bit more cooking liquid, a tablespoon at a time.

Mix and knead on low speed for about 5 minutes or until the dough is smooth and elastic. Transfer the dough to a lightly oiled bowl and cover with lightly oiled cling film. Leave to rise in a warm spot for about an hour or until doubled in size.

Turn out the risen dough on to a lightly floured surface and knead gently to knock out the large air bubbles. Divide the dough in half and shape each piece into a round loaf. Place the loaves on a lightly floured baking sheet and dust the tops with flour. Cover with oiled cling film and leave to prove in a warm spot until doubled in size.

Preheat the oven to 200°C/Fan 180°C/ Gas Mark 6. Remove the cling film and bake the loaves for 30–40 minutes or until they are golden brown and sound hollow when tapped on the underside. Cool on a wire rack. Store in a bread tin if not serving freshly baked.

BLACK PUDDING ROLLS

I got the idea for these rolls after having a lovely meal at a Spanish restaurant where they served some gorgeous chorizo bread with olive oil. I think this British version is just as delicious as the black pudding is properly embedded in the bread dough. It is a full-flavoured bread, which needs little else, except for a pat of good, unsalted butter.

MAKES 26–27 ROLLS OR 1 LARGE LOAF

500g strong white bread flour, plus
    extra for dusting
15g fine sea salt
2 x 7g sachets fast-action dried yeast
1 large egg, lightly beaten
550ml soured cream
200g black pudding, skin removed,
    then chopped or crumbled
flavourless oil for greasing
2 egg yolks beaten with 2 tablespoons
    milk, for glazing

Mix the flour, salt and yeast in the bowl of an electric mixer fitted with the dough hook. Make a well in the centre and tip in the egg and soured cream. Mix on low speed until the ingredients come together to make a dough that will come away from the sides of the bowl. If the dough seems very wet and tacky, add a little more flour and mix well, but do note that the dough should be quite soft and moist.

Add the black pudding and mix well. Increase the mixer speed to medium and knead the dough for about 5 minutes or until it looks smooth, save for the little lumps of black pudding. Transfer the dough to a lightly oiled bowl and cover with a lightly oiled piece of cling film. Leave to rise in a warm place for 1–2 hours or until doubled in size.

Knock back the dough and give it a light kneading on a lightly floured work surface. Divide into pieces about 50g in weight and shape into individual rolls. You could also roll out the dough to 2.5cm thickness and stamp out discs using a 5–6cm round pastry cutter. Arrange the rolls or discs, spaced well apart, on several oiled, large baking sheets. (If you want to make a loaf, shape the dough into a neat round and place on an oiled baking sheet.) Cover with oiled cling film and leave to rise for 1–2 hours or until doubled in size.

Preheat the oven to 220°C/Fan 200°C/ Gas Mark 7. Brush the rolls with the egg yolk glaze, then bake for 12–15 minutes or until they are golden brown (a loaf will take 30–40 minutes). They should feel light when you pick them up and sound hollow when tapped on the underside. Leave to cool for a few minutes, then transfer to a wire rack to cool completely.

ENGLISH MUFFINS

These English muffins are great to make in the height of summer, when it is too hot to fire up the oven. For me, there is nothing like a bacon butty made with a fresh English muffin, crisp grilled bacon and HP sauce – I would happily eat this for breakfast, lunch and dinner! It is also particularly good as a midnight snack after a night out, or as is often my case, after a busy dinner service.

MAKES 8 MUFFINS

300g strong white bread flour
7g sachet fast-action dried yeast
15g caster sugar
7g fine sea salt
15g unsalted butter, softened
1 large egg, lightly beaten
150ml whole milk
flavourless oil for greasing
25g semolina or polenta, for dusting

Put the flour, yeast, sugar and salt into the bowl of an electric mixer fitted with the dough hook. Give the mixture a stir and make a well in the middle. Add the butter, egg and milk to the well. Mix on low speed until the ingredients begin to come together to make a dough that will leave the sides of the bowl. If the dough seems dry, mix in a little more milk, a tablespoon at a time; if the dough seems too wet, add a little flour. The dough should be very soft and moist.

Increase the mixer speed to medium and knead the dough for about 5 minutes or until it is smooth and elastic. Transfer the dough to a lightly greased mixing bowl and cover with a lightly greased piece of cling film. Leave to rise in a warm spot for an hour or until the dough has doubled in size.

Dust a work surface with half of the semolina. Turn the dough out on to this, then roll out to 1.5cm thickness. Use a 9cm round pastry cutter to stamp out neat discs; re-roll the trimmings and stamp out more discs. Place them, spaced well apart, on a baking sheet lightly dusted with the remaining semolina. Cover with the oiled cling film and leave to rise for 30–40 minutes or until doubled in size.

Set a non-stick frying pan (or a wide, heavy-based griddle pan) over very low heat. Place the muffins in the hot pan, cover with a lid and cook for 5–6 minutes on each side or until golden brown. Serve while still warm.

BRIOCHE LOAF

A good homemade brioche tastes miles apart from the overly sweet and artificially softened commercial ones. It is very versatile and I find myself including it in almost every course at the restaurants: freshly toasted brioche slices are served with foie gras or chicken liver terrines; brioche breadcrumbs are used to top savoury crumbles; brioche batons accompany cheese fondues; and brioche croutons are used to garnish chocolate desserts. And, although tasty on its own with a little homemade jam, it also makes a delicious French toast for breakfast.

MAKES 3 SMALL LOAVES

295g strong white bread flour, plus extra for dusting
1 teaspoon fine sea salt
7g sachet fast-action dried yeast
40g caster sugar
45ml water
55ml tepid whole milk
2 medium eggs, lightly beaten
115g unsalted butter, softened, plus extra for greasing
1 large egg yolk beaten with 1 tablespoon milk, for glazing

Sift the flour and salt into the bowl of an electric mixer fitted with the dough hook. Stir in the yeast and sugar, then make a well in the centre. Add the water, milk and eggs to the well. Mix on the lowest speed until the ingredients start to come together. Add the butter and continue to mix to make a soft, sticky dough. Increase the mixer speed and knead for 3–4 minutes or until the dough is smooth and elastic and it will come cleanly off the sides of the mixer bowl. (If the dough seems too wet, mix in a little more flour, a tablespoon at a time.)

Cover the mixing bowl with a lightly oiled piece of cling film and leave the dough to rise in a warm spot for about an hour or until doubled in size. (You could also let the dough rise slowly in the fridge overnight, which will develop more flavour.)

Lightly grease and flour three 500g loaf tins. Knock back the risen dough by gently punching it down, then divide it into three equal pieces. Put one piece on a lightly floured work surface and divide into three portions. Shape each of these into a round ball, then place them in a row in a prepared loaf tin. Repeat to make the other two loaves. Lightly cover the loaves with oiled pieces of cling film, then leave to rise for 1–2 hours. The loaves are ready to be baked when little indentations are left if you gently press the dough with a finger.

Preheat the oven to 210°C/Fan 190°C/Gas Mark 7. Brush the top of each loaf with the egg yolk glaze, then bake for 15–20 minutes or until evenly brown. Remove from the oven and leave to cool for 5 minutes, then turn out on to a wire rack to cool completely. Brioche is best enjoyed while still warm but can be kept for 2–3 days. For longer storage (up to 6 weeks), wrap the brioche well and freeze.

Note

For this recipe, you could also make one large loaf in a loaf tin or individual buns but you will need to adjust the oven time accordingly: allow an extra 10–15 minutes for a large loaf, and reduce the baking time by about 5–10 minutes for individual buns. To freeze, wrap the brioche well then freeze and consume within 6 weeks.

BREADS & MUFFINS

FOUGASSE

This classic French bread is a stunner and even if your finished loaf does not really resemble the traditional leaf shape it will still have an appealingly rugged look. Do feel free to add different toppings to your fougasse – chopped herbs, pitted olives, sun-dried tomatoes, grated cheese and even caramelised onions are good choices.

MAKES 2 LOAVES

615g plain flour, plus extra for
   dusting
12g fine sea salt
12g fast-action dried yeast
15g unsalted butter, melted
55ml whole milk
85ml olive oil, plus extra for brushing
about 285ml tepid water
Maldon sea salt, for sprinkling
a few sprigs of rosemary, leaves
   picked

Sift the flour and salt together into the bowl of an electric mixer fitted with the dough hook. Add the yeast and mix well. Make a well in the centre of the dry ingredients and add the melted butter, milk, olive oil and 250ml of the water. Start mixing on low speed until a soft dough forms. If the dough looks a little dry, add another tablespoon of water and mix well. The dough should be very soft.

Increase the mixer speed to medium and knead the dough for 7–8 minutes or until it is smooth and elastic. Transfer it to a lightly oiled bowl and cover with a lightly oiled piece of cling film. Leave to rise in a warm spot for about an hour or until doubled in size.

Turn the dough out on to a lightly floured surface and give it a couple of folds. Divide the dough in half and pat out each piece into an oval shape. Lightly oil two baking sheets, then place a dough oval on each. Using a sharp knife, cut a few slashes in each oval like the spokes of a wheel, cutting to within 2–3cm of the edge. Gently pull the slashes apart until the dough oval roughly resembles a large leaf. Cover lightly with oiled cling film and leave to rise for an hour or until doubled in size.

Preheat the oven to 200°C/Fan 180°C/Gas Mark 6. Brush the dough with a light coating of olive oil, then sprinkle with a little Maldon sea salt and rosemary leaves. Place the baking sheets in the oven and spray with a little water to create some steam. Bake the fougasses for 15–20 minutes or until they are golden brown and sound hollow when tapped on the underside. Transfer to a wire rack and cool to warm or room temperature before serving.

SOURDOUGH

It is an understatement to say that making sourdough from scratch requires lots of patience and dedication. Although the process for making a sourdough is long, it is by no means complicated. At the core, all you need are the four basic ingredients of flour, water, salt and natural yeast cultivated from the air around you. It is this last ingredient that primarily gives sourdough bread its distinctive character. A famous San Franciscan sourdough, with its characteristic sourness, will taste remarkably different from a sourdough made in London. There are numerous other factors that will also affect the taste and texture of the finished loaf, but one could write a whole book just on this topic alone. For now, I urge you to try the recipe at least once, for the pride and satisfaction that you get from taking your first bite of a freshly baked homemade sourdough is indescribable.

MAKES 2 LOAVES, PLUS SOURDOUGH STARTER

For the starter
20g rye flour, plus 60g extra for feeding
20g strong white bread flour, plus 310g extra for feeding
50ml water, plus 350ml extra for feeding
20g natural yoghurt
20g raisins

For the sponge
450g strong white bread flour
225ml cold water

For the loaves
450g strong white bread flour
2 teaspoons fine sea salt
250ml cold water

To make the starter, combine the flours, water and yoghurt in a large container and stir to form a paste. Add the raisins and mix well. Cover the container tightly and leave the mixture to ferment in a relatively warm place overnight. (The ideal temperature for a starter is 20–21°C.)

On day 2, 'feed' the starter by stirring in another 20g each of rye and white flours and 50ml of water. (You may now be able to see a few bubbles in the starter mixture and it might have a mild yeasty fragrance. However, do not worry if your starter is slow to activate – it should be bubbling after another day or two of feeding.) Cover the container and leave to ferment overnight.

On day 3, your starter may be looking bubbly and frothy. It may also smell a little sour and musty. Add 100ml of water to the starter and mix well. Strain the watery mixture through a sieve to remove and discard the raisins, then add 40g each of rye and white flours and stir until smooth. Cover the container and leave to ferment for another day.

On day 4, give the starter a quick stir. It should have increased in volume slightly and have a mixture of large and small bubbles, and it should have a sour, pungent smell. Measure out half of the starter and discard the rest. Add 125g white flour and 100ml water to the measured starter and stir until smooth. Cover the container and leave overnight.

On day 5, stir the starter well and repeat the process from day 4 (discard half of the starter and feed the remainder with 125g white flour and 100ml water). Cover and leave to ferment overnight.

On day 6, give the starter a stir. It should have increased in volume, smell pleasantly sour and yeasty, and look frothy with both large and small bubbles. You can now use it to prepare a sponge for making bread the next day. To do this, measure out 225g of the starter into a large bowl and add the flour and water for the sponge. (Save the leftover starter for future loaves or give it away to a friend; see note below on how to maintain a starter.) Mix the ingredients together to form a firm dough, then loosely cover the bowl with a clean tea towel. Leave to ferment overnight.

On day 7, to make the loaves, measure out 225g of the sponge and put it into the bowl of an electric mixer fitted with the dough hook. (You can give the leftover sponge away or save it to use another day.) Add the flour, salt and water and mix on low speed for a few minutes or until the ingredients come together to make a dough that is soft but not too sticky. If you find it too dry, add a little more water. Increase the mixer speed to medium and knead the dough for about 5 minutes or until it is smooth and elastic. It should spring back when you prod it with a finger.

(continued on page 30

BREADS & MUFFINS

Transfer the dough to a lightly oiled bowl and cover with a lightly oiled piece of cling film. Leave to rise in a warm spot for about an hour or until the dough has doubled in volume. (Sourdough takes a bit longer to rise than conventional bread dough made with commercial yeast, so be patient.) For even more flavour, you could let the dough rise slowly in the fridge overnight.

Knock back the dough and give it a few folds. Divide the dough in half and shape each piece into a neat round or oval-shaped loaf. Place the loaves on a large baking sheet that is lightly dusted with flour. Or put them to rise in baker's proving baskets that have been generously dusted with flour. Cover the loaves with oiled cling film and leave to rise in a warm place for a few hours or until doubled in size (if you gently prod them with a finger, an indentation should be left).

Towards the end of the rising time, preheat the oven to 230°C/Fan 210°C/Gas Mark 8. Have ready a spray bottle filled with water. If you have used baker's proving baskets, tip the loaves on to a lightly floured baking sheet. Dust the top of each loaf with a little more flour, then slash a couple of times with a sharp knife or razor blade.

Put the loaves into the hot oven and spray the tops and sides with a little water, then quickly close the oven door. Bake for 15 minutes. Reduce the heat to 200°C/Fan 180°C/Gas Mark 6 and give the loaves another spray, then continue to bake for 10–15 minutes or until the loaves are brown and they sound hollow when you tap them on the underside.

Remove from the oven and leave to cool completely on a wire rack. The loaves will keep well in a bread tin for a week. Should you find that any slices are becoming stale, simply toast to refresh them or use them to make tasty croutons or sourdough breadcrumbs.

Maintaining a Sourdough Starter
Once you've successfully made a loaf of sourdough, chances are you want to keep the starter for future bakes. Maintaining a starter is by no means difficult but you do need to bear in mind that it is a living culture that requires regular feeding.

If making bread is a daily ritual in your household, you may want to keep the sourdough starter in a jar or sealable container at room temperature, ready to make bread at a moment's notice. You would need to feed it regularly – some bakers recommend twice-a-day feedings, particularly in the hot summer months when the yeast is more active.

For less frequent baking, keep the starter in the fridge and feed it once a week. I find it best to let the starter come to room temperature before feeding it because this gives the yeast a chance to 'wake up'. If there is a layer of clear liquid on top of the starter, simply pour this off before giving the mixture a stir.

Each time you feed, repeat the procedure described above for days 4 and 5. (It might seem wasteful to discard part of your starter, but this is necessary to balance the ph levels of the mixture. And it is easier to manage smaller amounts. You can, of course, give away the starter

you don't need.) If you're keeping your starter in the fridge, let it rest at room temperature for 2 hours before returning to the fridge. I would also recommend that you feed the starter every day for 2 days before you intend to use it for baking.

If you are going away on holiday, or simply want to take a long break from baking, you can freeze the starter. Divide into several portions, wrap in cling film and store in the freezer for several months. When you feel like baking, take out a portion and let it thaw at room temperature, then feed with flour and tepid water. As before, give the starter a few days of feeding before you use it for baking.

PAIN D'ÉPICES

This fragrant, dense and moist French gingerbread is traditionally served with cheese plates, foie gras and carbonnade, a Flemish sweet and sour stew made with beef, onions and ale. The spiced bread is lovely on its own but I also use it to make a sweet tartine with soft cheese and figs (see page 222). Due to the high honey content, pain d'épices can keep well for over a week in an airtight container.

MAKES 1 LOAF

115g honey
200ml water
20ml dark or light rum
2 star anise
1 clove
120g mixed dried fruit
finely grated zest of 1 lemon
finely grated zest of 1 orange
flavourless oil for greasing
75g golden caster sugar
85g ground almonds
2 teaspoons bicarbonate of soda
¼ teaspoon fine sea salt
1 teaspoon mixed spice
225g plain flour, sifted

Put the honey, water, rum, star anise and clove into a small saucepan and give the mixture a stir. Bring to the boil, then immediately remove from the heat and allow the syrup to cool completely. Strain the cooled syrup through a fine sieve into a large bowl (discard the spices), then add the dried fruit and lemon and orange zests. Mix well. Leave the fruit to soak in the spiced syrup for about an hour.

Preheat the oven to 160°C/Fan 140°C/Gas Mark 3. Grease a 900g loaf tin and line with baking parchment. Combine the rest of the ingredients in a large mixing bowl and make a well in the centre. Pour in the soaked fruits and syrup, then fold the ingredients together. Transfer the mixture to the prepared loaf tin and level the top with a spatula.

Bake for about 1 hour or until a skewer inserted into the centre of the loaf comes out clean. Remove from the oven and leave the pain d'épices to cool for 10 minutes before unmoulding on to a wire rack to cool. Keep in a bread tin and enjoy for a week.

CHOCOLATE CHIP MUFFINS

These chocolate chip muffins aren't as cloyingly sweet as the ones you would find in the shops, making them ideal for breakfast. To make them a little healthier, replace a third of the flour with wholemeal flour or fine oatmeal and add a handful of chopped pecans or walnuts to the batter.

MAKES 12 LARGE MUFFINS

80g unsalted butter, softened
120g caster sugar
250g plain flour
30g cocoa powder
1 tablespoon baking powder
2 large eggs
215ml whole milk
1 teaspoon vanilla extract
150g dark chocolate chips

Preheat the oven to 180°C/Fan 160°C/ Gas Mark 4. Line a 12-hole muffin tin with paper muffin cases.

Put the butter and sugar into a large mixing bowl and beat with an electric whisk until the mixture is pale, light and fluffy. Sift together the flour, cocoa powder and baking powder. In another bowl, beat together the eggs, milk and vanilla extract. Fold half of the flour mixture into the butter mixture, then fold through half of the egg mixture. Repeat until all the wet and dry mixtures have been incorporated. Finally, fold in the chocolate chips until evenly distributed.

Spoon the muffin batter into the paper cases. Bake for 12–15 minutes or until a skewer inserted into the middle of a muffin comes out clean. Leave to cool for a few minutes in the tin, then transfer the muffins to a wire rack to cool completely before serving.

CORNBREAD MUFFINS

Sweet and salty cornbread is an American import that has gained popularity in recent years, with the multitude of barbecue and rib joints that have opened up all over London. These are lovely with barbecues (yes!) and chilli con carne but we also often eat them for breakfast as a change to the usual butter on toast.

MAKES ABOUT 16 LARGE MUFFINS

130g unsalted butter, softened
60g caster sugar
2 large eggs, lightly beaten
175g plain flour
1 teaspoon fine sea salt
1 tablespoon baking powder
175g fine polenta or semolina
350ml whole milk
125g drained canned sweetcorn

Preheat the oven to 180°C/Fan 160°C/ Gas Mark 4. Line a 12-hole muffin tin with paper muffin cases. (If you want to make mini muffins, line two 12-hole mini muffin tins with mini muffin cases.)

In a large mixing bowl, cream together the butter and sugar until light and fluffy. Gradually beat in the eggs (if the mixture threatens to curdle, beat in a tablespoon of the flour). Sift the flour, salt, baking powder and polenta into the bowl and fold through. Finally, fold in the milk and sweetcorn.

Spoon the mixture into the muffin cases to three-quarters fill them. Bake large muffins for 15–20 minutes, mini muffins for 10–12 minutes, or until a skewer inserted into the middle comes out clean. Leave to cool for a few minutes before transferring to a wire rack to cool completely.

BREADS & MUFFINS

BISCUITS

BISCUITS

CHEDDAR CHEESE SHORTBREAD

These cheese biscuits make a delicious snack but we also offer them as part of a cheese platter alongside a pot of good chutney. For an easy and delicious canapé, use the cheddar shortbread as a base for smoked salmon or smoked mackerel pâté. The unbaked dough freezes well so if you don't need a large batch of cheese shortbread, bake half the recipe and save the remaining dough for another time.

MAKES 35–45 BISCUITS

200g unsalted butter, softened
2 large egg yolks
300g plain flour
1 teaspoon fine sea salt
a pinch of freshly ground black
   pepper
finely grated zest of 1 lemon
¼ teaspoon finely chopped rosemary
120g mature Cheddar cheese, grated

In a large mixing bowl, lightly beat together the butter and egg yolks. Sift in the flour and salt, then add the rest of the ingredients. Mix until everything comes together into a dough. Divide the dough in half. Put one half on a large piece of cling film. Fold the cling film over the dough and roll back and forth to shape into a long log, about 4cm in diameter. Wrap in the cling film, twisting the ends like a Christmas cracker. Holding both ends, roll the log on the work surface to even out the thickness. Repeat with the second half of the dough. Refrigerate the logs for at least an hour.

Preheat the oven to 160°C/Fan 140°C /Gas Mark 3. Line one or two large baking sheets with silicone mats or baking parchment. Unwrap the dough logs and cut across into 1cm thick discs. Arrange them on the baking sheets, leaving 4–5cm of space between each disc. Bake for 10–15 minutes or until the shortbread rounds are light golden brown around the edges.

Remove from the oven and leave the biscuits to cool for a few minutes before transferring to a wire rack. Once completely cooled, keep them in an airtight container and enjoy within 1–2 weeks.

BISCUITS

PARMESAN AND BLACK OLIVE BISCUITS

These Mediterranean-inspired biscuits are fantastic with aperitifs and they go really well with a glass of sparkling wine, Prosecco or Kir Royale. We tend to make big batches of these over the Christmas period as they are great to whip out when unexpected guests arrive.

MAKES 25–35 BISCUITS

205g plain flour, plus extra for
    dusting
½ teaspoon fine sea salt
½ teaspoon cayenne pepper
⅔ teaspoon English mustard powder
75g Parmesan cheese, finely grated
185g unsalted butter, softened
50g pitted black olives, finely chopped

Sift the flour, salt, cayenne pepper and mustard powder into a large mixing bowl. Stir in the grated Parmesan, then add the softened butter and mix well with a wooden spoon. The mixture may seem a little dry at first but carry on mixing and the dough will eventually come together. Add the chopped olives and mix into the dough until evenly distributed.

Tip the dough on to a large piece of cling film. Fold the film over the dough, then roll back and forth on the work surface to shape into a neat log 4–5cm in diameter. Wrap in the cling film, twisting the ends like a Christmas cracker. Holding both ends, roll the log on the work surface to even out the thickness. Refrigerate for at least 30 minutes so the dough can rest and firm up slightly. (At this point, you can freeze the dough, to slice and bake at a later time.)

When ready to bake, preheat the oven to 180°C/Fan 160°C/Gas Mark 4. Unwrap the dough log and slice across into 1cm thick discs. Arrange them on a couple of large baking sheets lined with silicone mats or baking parchment. Bake for 7–10 minutes or until golden brown. Remove from the oven and leave to cool completely on the baking sheets; the biscuits will crisp up as they cool. Store in an airtight container and enjoy within a week.

BROWNIES

These irresistible brownies are one of the elements to our House Mississippi Mud Slide sundae (see page 107) but they are also absolutely scrumptious on their own. It is crucial to avoid over-baking the brownies in order to retain the moist, fudgy texture. To make black and white brownies, stir 100g of white chocolate chips (or chopped white chocolate) through the batter just before you spread it in the tin.

MAKES 16 BROWNIES

225g dark chocolate (with about 60% cocoa solids)
150g unsalted butter, diced, plus extra melted butter for greasing
150g caster sugar
2 large eggs
75g plain flour
a pinch of fine sea salt
⅛ teaspoon baking powder
⅛ teaspoon bicarbonate of soda
100g walnuts, roughly chopped

Break the chocolate into small pieces and place in a large heatproof bowl. Add the diced butter. Set the bowl over a saucepan of gently simmering water (make sure the base of the bowl does not touch the water) and stir the chocolate and butter until melted and smooth. Take the bowl off the pan and leave to cool.

Preheat the oven to 180°C/Fan 160°C/ Gas Mark 4. Grease a 15 x 20cm baking tray or a 20cm square cake tin and line with baking parchment. Put the sugar and eggs into the bowl of an electric mixer and beat on high speed until the mixture is pale and light and has tripled in volume. Sift together the flour, salt, baking powder and bicarbonate of soda. Fold the melted chocolate into the egg mixture, followed by the flour and walnuts.

Spread the mixture in the prepared tray or tin. Bake for 25–35 minutes or until the brownie cake has set around the edges but is still slightly under-baked in the centre – after the initial 20 minutes of baking, check every 5 minutes by inserting a skewer into the middle. When the brownie cake is done the skewer will come out with moist crumbs adhering to it but not sticky, wet batter. (If the skewer comes out clean, the brownie will still be delicious, but will not have a moist, fudgy centre.)

Leave to cool completely before lifting the brownie cake out of the tray or tin, using the baking parchment to help. (The top will crack if you try to unmould it while it is still warm). Cut into squares for serving. You can keep the brownies in an airtight tin for a couple of weeks, or for a month in the freezer.

Variation
To make Black and White Brownies, stir 100g of white chocolate chips (or chopped white chocolate) through the mixture just before you spread it in the tin.

BISCUITS

CHOCOLATE AND FLEUR DE SEL SABLÉS

Ever since I worked with Ferran Adria at El Bulli, I have always added a bit of sea salt to my chocolate recipes to really enhance the flavours of the chocolate. I consider these short chocolate sables the posh French cousins of American chocolate cookies. At the restaurants, we sometimes serve them with coffee as part of our petit four selection.

MAKES 40–45 BISCUITS

185g dark chocolate (with about 70% cocoa solids)
215g plain flour
40g cocoa powder
1 teaspoon bicarbonate of soda
185g unsalted butter
150g soft light brown sugar
60g caster sugar
½ teaspoon fleur de sel (or Maldon sea salt)
½ teaspoon vanilla extract

Chop the chocolate into small pieces and set aside. Sift the flour, cocoa powder and bicarbonate of soda into a large bowl.

In another large bowl, cream the butter with the brown and caster sugars, the fleur de sel and vanilla extract until light and fluffy. Fold in the flour mixture, followed by the chopped chocolate. Gather the dough into a disc and wrap in cling film. Refrigerate for at least 30 minutes or until firm.

Preheat the oven to 180°C/Fan 160°C/ Gas Mark 4. Line two baking sheets with silicone mats or baking parchment. Roll out the dough on a lightly floured work surface to 1cm thickness. Use a small pastry cutter, about 5cm in diameter, to stamp out neat discs of dough. Arrange these on the baking sheets, spacing them slightly apart. Bake for about 10 minutes or until golden brown around the edges. Leave the biscuits to cool completely before storing in an airtight container. They can be kept for up to a week.

CHOCOLATE CHIP COOKIES

These super-charged cookies are truly loaded with chocolate chips – a real treat for chocoholics! The recipe makes quite a generous amount (which is ideal for bake sales), but if you prefer not to bake as many at a time, shape half of the unbaked dough into a log, wrap well with cling film and keep in the fridge for up to a week (or freeze for up to 6 weeks). Cut into thick slices and bake whenever you want freshly baked cookies. They can be baked from frozen but allow for a couple of extra minutes of baking time.

MAKES 18–20 LARGE COOKIES OR 52–54 SMALLER ONES

380g plain flour
2 teaspoons bicarbonate of soda
1 teaspoon fine sea salt
210g unsalted butter, softened
170g soft dark brown sugar
170g caster sugar
1 teaspoon vanilla extract
3 large eggs, at room temperature, lightly beaten
300g chocolate chips

Sift together the flour, bicarbonate of soda and salt and set aside. Put the butter, brown sugar, caster sugar and vanilla extract into the bowl of an electric mixer and beat for about a minute until the mixture is light and creamy. Gradually add the eggs, beating well. With the mixer on low speed, beat in the flour mixture until just incorporated. Finally, add the chocolate chips and stir in until they are evenly distributed throughout the dough.

Using a large ice-cream scoop or a large spoon, scoop out 75g portions of dough and place them, spaced about 5cm apart, on two to three large baking sheets lined with silicone mats or baking parchment. (To make smaller cookies, use a mini ice-cream scoop to measure out 25–30g balls.) Place the baking sheets in the freezer and chill for 30–60 minutes so the cookies firm up a little.

When ready to bake, preheat the oven to 170°C/Fan 150°C/Gas Mark 3. Bake large cookies for 15–18 minutes, smaller ones for 10–13 minutes, or until they are golden brown around the edges but the centres are still a little soft. Remove from the oven and leave the cookies to cool for a few minutes to firm up, then transfer to wire racks to cool completely. Store them in an airtight container and enjoy within a week.

CHOCOLATE-COATED HONEYCOMB

This is our fun take on the Crunchie bar and it never fails to light up children's faces. We have also served little morsels of these chocolate honeycombs as petit fours at the restaurant and they proved to be very popular with our guests, regardless of their age.

SERVES 8–10

**flavourless oil or melted butter, for greasing
130g caster sugar
20g runny honey
20ml water
50g liquid glucose
4g bicarbonate of soda
100g dark chocolate (with at least 60% cocoa solids), chopped**

Lightly grease a 20cm square cake tin. Put the sugar, honey, water and liquid glucose into a heavy-based pan and set over medium heat. Give the mixture a quick stir, then let the sugar dissolve slowly, swirling it in the pan now and again. Once all the sugar has dissolved, increase the heat to high and boil the syrup vigorously until it begins to turn to an amber-coloured caramel.

As soon as the mixture has started to caramelise, take the pan off the heat and tip in the bicarbonate of soda. Immediately beat the soda into the caramel using a heatproof spatula until the mixture is foaming. Quickly pour and scrape the honeycomb mixture into the greased tin, taking care not to get any of the piping hot mixture on your hands. Gently tilt the tin from side to side to even out the honeycomb, then leave to cool and set for about an hour. Once the honeycomb has hardened, use the tip of a knife to break it into large pieces.

Melt the chocolate in a heatproof bowl set over a pan of gently simmering water, stirring until smooth. Remove from the heat. Coat the honeycomb pieces in the melted chocolate (dip them in, or hold over the bowl of chocolate and spoon it over them), then set them on a baking sheet lined with a silicone mat and leave to set. When the chocolate has hardened, store the honeycomb in an airtight container, with sheets of baking parchment between each layer. To serve, I like to cut the chocolate-covered pieces in half to show off the honeycomb.

ENGLISH SCONES

The key to making light scones is to use cold butter and to work quickly to avoid getting the butter too soft. When combining the ingredients together, you do not need to knead the dough until it is silky smooth – it just needs to come together in a ball.

MAKES ABOUT 14 SMALL SCONES

225g plain flour, plus extra for
    dusting
1 tablespoon baking powder
50g cold unsalted butter, diced
50g caster sugar
25g sultanas, soaked in a little milk or
    hot water to plump
150ml whole milk
150ml double cream
1 large egg
1 large egg yolk mixed with 1
    tablespoon water, for glazing

Preheat the oven to 220°C/Fan 200°C/ Gas Mark 7. Dust a large baking sheet with a little flour. Sift the measured flour and baking powder into a large mixing bowl. Add the butter and rub into the flour with the tips of your fingers until the mixture resemble fine crumbs. Stir in the sugar.

Drain the sultanas and add to the bowl. Stir to mix, then make a well in the centre. Lightly whisk together the milk, cream and egg, then pour this mixture into the well. Using a table knife or rubber/plastic spatula, quickly mix until it all comes together into a soft, sticky dough.

Dust some flour on a work surface and tip out the dough on to this. Dredge the dough and your hands with a little more flour, then fold the dough over several times until it is a little smoother. Pat out the dough with your hands until it is about 4cm thick. Dust a 5cm round pastry cutter with a little flour, then use it to stamp out neat discs of dough. (When stamping out, try not to twist the cutter or the scones will rise unevenly during baking.) Gather up the dough trimmings and give them a few folds to combine, then flatten and stamp out more discs. Arrange the scones on a baking sheet, leaving a bit of space around each one.

Brush the tops of the scones with the egg yolk glaze, then bake for 10–15 minutes or until risen and golden brown on top. Remove from the oven and leave to cool. The scones are best eaten freshly baked and generously filled with clotted cream and jam. Once cooled, they can be frozen on the day of baking; thaw before serving, then cut the scones in half and toast them, or reheat in a 140°C/Fan 120°C/Gas Mark 2 oven.

BISCUITS

SOCIAL SWEETS

MADELEINES

When I started cooking professionally, madeleines were one of the first few recipes I learnt to master. For this, it really pays to invest in a couple of good, non-stick madeleine pans. The secret to getting the characteristic dome on the wider end is to let the madeleine batter stand for about 15–20 minutes, just as you would a pancake batter. However, there is no need to fret if your madeleines do not rise as dramatically; they will taste just as delicious.

MAKES 15–16 LARGE MADELEINES OR 47–48 MINI ONES

125g unsalted butter, plus extra for greasing
110g plain flour, plus extra for the moulds
2 large eggs
90g caster sugar
15g demerara sugar
20g runny honey
1 vanilla pod, split in half, seeds scraped out with a knife
½ teaspoon baking powder

Melt the butter in a small saucepan, then set aside to cool. Brush two madeleine trays (or four 12-hole mini madeleine trays) with a little melted butter, then dust with a little flour, tipping out any excess. (If you have only one madeleine tray, bake in batches.)

Whisk the eggs with the caster and demerara sugars until the mixture is light and frothy. Add the honey, vanilla seeds and cooled melted butter, then whisk again to mix. Sift the flour and baking powder over the top and fold in until well incorporated. Leave to stand for 15–20 minutes.

Preheat the oven to 200°C/Fan 180°C/Gas Mark 6. Spoon the batter into the prepared madeleine trays. Bake large madeleines for 8–10 minutes, mini ones for 4–6 minutes, or until golden brown around the edges and risen and peaked in the middle. Transfer the madeleines to a wire rack and leave to cool slightly before serving. They are best eaten freshly baked but will keep for a few days in an airtight container.

FINANCIERS

When I first opened Pollen Street Social, I thought it would be a nice touch to offer our guests a little goody bag of sweet treats to take home after their meal to enjoy for breakfast. These gorgeous financiers were one of the things we gave away. They are addictive and I can't tell you how many times people have asked me for the recipe.

MAKES ABOUT 24 FINANCIERS

100g unsalted butter, plus extra for greasing
20g plain flour, plus extra for the moulds
100g finely ground almonds
150g caster sugar
4 large egg whites
100g Raspberry Jam (see page 245)

Put the butter in a saucepan and set it over medium heat. Let the butter melt, without stirring, then continue to heat for 5–7 minutes until it turns a nutty brown colour. Be careful not to let it burn, which can happen quite quickly once it begins to colour. When ready, strain the butter through a fine sieve into a bowl and leave to cool completely.

Preheat the oven to 200°C/Fan 180°C/Gas Mark 6. Grease and flour two 12-hole mini muffin tins (or 24 barquette moulds). Combine the flour, ground almonds and sugar in a large mixing bowl and make a well in the centre. Pour the cooled browned butter into the well. In another bowl, lightly beat the egg whites until frothy, then add to the large bowl. Fold the wet ingredients through the dry ones. Spoon the mixture into the prepared tins to half fill each mould.

Stir the raspberry jam to loosen it, then spoon it into a small piping bag fitted with a thin, long nozzle. Pipe a small amount of jam (a scant half teaspoonful) into the centre of the mixture in each mould. Lightly tap the tins on the work surface once or twice to level the mixture.

Bake for 10–15 minutes or until the financiers are golden brown around the edges. Remove from the oven and leave to cool for a few minutes before unmoulding. (You may need to use the tip of a knife or small offset spatula to release the financiers from the moulds.) Transfer them to a wire rack to cool completely. The financiers are best served on the same day but you can keep them for a few days in an airtight container.

BISCUITS

SCOTTISH SHORTBREAD

In my mind, this is the perfect shortbread recipe as it has just the right amount of butter and the biscuits turn out lovely and short. In addition to the vanilla, a little orange zest gives it a lovely mild fragrance. For added indulgence, you could half coat the shortbread rounds in dark chocolate. To do so, simply dip half of each shortbread in melted chocolate and leave it to set on a baking sheet lined with baking parchment or a silicone mat.

MAKES 45–46 BISCUITS

325g unsalted butter, softened, plus extra for greasing
150g caster sugar, plus extra for sprinkling
500g plain flour
8g fine sea salt
finely grated zest of ½ orange
½ vanilla pod, split in half, seeds scraped out with a knife

Put the butter and sugar into a large mixing bowl and beat with a wooden spoon until the mixture is smooth. Sift in the flour and salt, then add the orange zest and vanilla seeds. Stir to combine, then press the mixture together with your hands to form a dough. Wrap the dough in cling film and chill for 15–20 minutes to allow it to firm up a little.

Preheat the oven to 190°C/Fan 170°C/Gas Mark 5. Unwrap the dough and gently roll it out on a lightly floured surface to 1cm thickness. (Bear in mind that the less you handle the dough, the 'shorter' and more crumbly the texture of the shortbread will be.) Stamp out neat discs with a 5cm round pastry cutter and arrange on two lightly greased, large baking sheets. Sprinkle the shortbread discs with caster sugar.

Bake for 15–18 minutes or until pale golden brown and just cooked through. Leave the shortbread to cool on the baking sheets for a few minutes, then transfer to a wire rack to cool completely. Store in an airtight container and enjoy within a week.

PEANUT BRITTLE

Many people buy commercially made peanut brittle but it is incredibly easy to make at home. All you need to do is caramelise some sugar and mix it with a smidge of butter and some roasted peanuts. I find that the brittle can become sticky over time, particularly if the weather is hot and humid, so it is better to make small amounts at a time to consume within a few days.

SERVES 6–8

25g unsalted butter, plus extra for greasing
120g toasted skinned peanuts
200g caster sugar
100ml water

Grease a 20cm square baking tin. Tip in the toasted peanuts and spread them out evenly.

Put the sugar and water into a heavy-based saucepan and stir over medium heat until the sugar has dissolved. Increase the heat to high and let the sugar syrup boil vigorously, without stirring, until it begins to caramelise.

When the caramel has turned a rich amber colour, take the pan off the heat and add the butter (take care as the hot caramel will spit and splutter when it comes into contact with the cold butter). Stir the mixture to combine. If there are any hardened bits of caramel, return the pan to the heat and stir until they have melted and the buttery caramel sauce is smooth.

Immediately pour the caramel over the peanuts in the tin. Leave to cool completely by which time the caramel will have set and hardened. Break into small shards, either with your hands or using the tip of a knife. Enjoy immediately or store in an airtight container for a couple of days.

classics

classics

MARCO'S LEMON TART

I have travelled to all corners of the globe and savoured many delicious desserts, but of all the lemon tarts I've tried, the top award still belongs to Marco Pierre White. I learnt to make his ultimate lemon tart early in my career when I worked at Harvey's in Wandsworth. It is superior in every way!

MAKES A DEEP 20CM TART TO SERVE 8

½ quantity Sweet Pastry (see page 239)
195g caster sugar
5 medium eggs
finely grated zest and juice of 3 large lemons
250ml double cream
sifted icing sugar, for dusting (optional)

Roll out the pastry on a lightly floured surface to the thickness of a £1 coin. Use to line a 20cm round tart tin that is 4–5cm deep with a removable base, lightly pressing the pastry smoothly over the base and up the sides of the tin; leave about 1cm of excess pastry hanging over the rim of the tin. Cover with a piece of cling film and chill in the freezer for 30 minutes or until firm.

Preheat the oven to 190°C/Fan 170°C/Gas Mark 5. Remove the cling film from the tart case and line it with baking parchment, then fill with baking beans. Blind bake for 15 minutes or until the sides of the case are set and lightly golden brown. Remove the beans and baking parchment, then return the pastry case to the oven to bake for a further 5 minutes or until the base is cooked through with no uncooked grey patches. Remove from the oven and carefully trim off the excess pastry around the rim with a sharp knife; set aside. Turn the oven down to 120°C/Fan 100°C/Gas Mark ½.

For the lemon filling, whisk together the sugar and eggs in a large bowl. Add the lemon zest and juice and stir well. Pour in the cream and mix until thoroughly combined. Transfer the filling to a large jug, then pour enough into the baked tart case until it is half full. Carefully transfer the tart to the pulled-out bottom shelf of the oven (make sure that the tart is kept level), then pour in the rest of the lemon filling until it reaches the top of the tart case. Gently slide the oven shelf back into the oven and bake the tart for 30–40 minutes or until the filling is set around the edges but still has a slight wobble in the middle when you gently move the tin.

Leave the tart to cool for at least 1½ hours, then dust with icing sugar before serving.

APPLE TARTE FINE

When I worked with Nico Ladenis at Chez Nico, I was responsible for making French apple tarts and they had to turn out perfectly or Nico would make me start them over. After thousands of apple tarts, I could make them in my sleep! Of course, nothing beats a good homemade puff pastry but if you decide to use a shop-bought all butter version then half the work is done for you. It is really then just an assembly job, layering the apples slices neatly on the puff pastry.

SERVES 6–8

50g unsalted butter, melted and
    cooled
50g caster sugar
300g Quick Puff Pastry (see page 238)
    or bought butter puff pastry
3 eating apples (such as Pink Lady,
    Jazz, Braeburn or Royal Gala)
sifted icing sugar, for dusting
    (optional)

Preheat the oven to 180°C/Fan 160°C/ Gas Mark 4. Line two large baking sheets with silicone mats or baking parchment. Brush the lined sheets with a little of the melted butter, then sprinkle over half of the caster sugar. Set aside.

Divide the pastry in half. On a lightly floured work surface, roll out each piece to 2–3mm thickness. Place the pastry bases on the buttered and sugared baking sheets. Keep the baking sheets in the fridge while you prepare the apples.

Peel and core the apples, then cut into neat 3mm slices. Remove the pastry bases from the fridge and arrange the apple slices on top, in overlapping rows, making sure that you leave a 1.5cm margin clear around the pastry rim. Brush the apples generously with melted butter, then sprinkle over the remaining caster sugar.

Bake the tart for 30–35 minutes or until the apples are cooked: there should be no resistance when you pierce them with the tip of a knife. (If the apple topping has not browned enough, sprinkle with a little extra caster sugar and place under a hot grill for 1–2 minutes – watching closely – until the sugar caramelises and the top is nicely golden brown.) Cool completely before cutting into slices and dusting with icing sugar.

BAKEWELL TART

I spent my early years in Sheffield, not far from the town of Bakewell, so I naturally have a soft spot for a good bakewell tart. Here, I'm using traditional raspberry jam in the filling but I have also made some pretty good bakewell tarts layered with gooseberry or damson jams.

MAKES A 23–24CM TART TO SERVE 8–10

250g Sweet Pastry (see page 239)
warm apricot jam, for glazing
sifted icing sugar, for dusting
  (optional)

For the filling
125g unsalted butter, softened
125g caster sugar
2 large eggs
125g ground almonds
25g plain flour
3 tablespoons Raspberry Jam (see
  page 245)
50g flaked almonds

On a lightly floured work surface, roll out the pastry to the thickness of a £1 coin. Gently roll the pastry over the rolling pin, then lay it over a 23–24cm round tart tin with a removable base. Line the tin with the pastry, smoothly pressing it over the base and up the sides; leave about 1cm of excess pastry hanging over the rim of the tin. Cover with cling film and chill in the freezer for at least an hour to let the pastry firm up.

Preheat the oven to 200°C/Fan 180°C/Gas Mark 6. Take the pastry case out of the freezer and remove the cling film. Line with baking parchment, then fill with baking beans. Blind bake for about 15 minutes or until the sides are lightly golden brown. Remove the baking beans and parchment, then return to the oven to bake for a further 5 minutes or until the pastry is lightly golden with no grey patches of uncooked pastry. Remove from the oven and trim off the excess pastry round the rim with a sharp knife. Set the pastry case aside. Lower the oven temperature to 180°C/Fan 160°C/Gas Mark 4.

For the filling, lightly beat together the butter and sugar until light and fluffy, then beat in the eggs. Add the ground almonds and flour and fold through until evenly combined.

Spread a thin layer of raspberry jam over the base of the tart case, then fill it with the almond mixture. Sprinkle the flaked almonds evenly on top. Bake the tart for 25–35 minutes or until the top is golden brown. Leave to cool slightly before brushing the top with warm apricot jam, then leave to cool completely. Dust with icing sugar before serving.

TRIPLE CHOCOLATE TART

No chocolate lover would be able resist this triple chocolate tart. It is very rich and indulgent so a little goes a long way.

MAKES A 24CM TART TO SERVE 12–16

½ **quantity Chocolate Sweet Pastry (see page 239)**
400g dark chocolate (with about 65% cocoa solids), chopped
45g milk chocolate, chopped
585ml whipping cream
95g runny honey

On a lightly floured surface, roll out the chocolate pastry to the thickness of a £1 coin. Gently roll the pastry over the rolling pin, then lay it over a 24cm round, deep tart tin with a removable base. Press the pastry smoothly over the base and up the sides of the tin, leaving about 1cm of excess pastry hanging over the edge. Cover with cling film and chill in the freezer for at least 30 minutes to allow the pastry to firm up.

Preheat the oven to 190°C/Fan 170°C/ Gas Mark 5. Remove the cling film and line the tart case with baking parchment. Fill with baking beans. Blind bake for 15 minutes or until the edges are set. Remove the baking beans and parchment and return the tart case to the oven to bake for a further 5 minutes or until the pastry is just cooked through. Remove from the oven and trim off the excess pastry around the rim of the tin with a sharp knife. Set aside.

For the filling, put the chopped dark and milk chocolates into a large heatproof bowl; set aside. Put the cream and honey into a saucepan and stir over medium heat until the honey has liquefied. Increase the heat slightly and bring to the boil. As soon as the mixture begins to bubble, take the pan off the heat.

Gradually add the hot cream mixture to the chopped chocolate, stirring until the mixture is smooth. Leave to cool to room temperature, then pour into the baked tart case. Without moving the tart, allow the filling to start to set for about an hour before transferring to the fridge. Chill for a few hours or until completely set. Remove the tart from the tin and let it come to room temperature before serving.

CUSTARD TART

Plain as it looks, a good custard tart is unrivalled as far as comfort puddings are concerned. In fact, top chefs like Marcus Wareing are still serving it in their fancy, Michelin-starred restaurants. To get the perfect soft and smooth texture, the custard should be slightly undercooked and wobbly when you take it out of the oven. It will continue to set in the residual heat. A generous grating of fresh nutmeg is a must!

MAKES A DEEP 20CM TART TO SERVE 8

275g Sweet Pastry (see page 239)
1 medium egg yolk, lightly beaten
385ml whipping cream
6 large egg yolks
50g caster sugar
1 fresh nutmeg, for grating

On a lightly floured work surface, roll out the pastry to the thickness of a £1 coin. Gently roll the pastry over the rolling pin, then lay it over a 20cm round tart tin that is 4cm deep with a removable base. Line the tin with the pastry, smoothly pressing it over the base and up the sides. Trim off the excess pastry, leaving 1–2cm hanging over the rim of the tin. Cover with cling film and rest in the fridge for at least 20 minutes to let the pastry firm up. This will help to reduce shrinkage during baking.

Preheat the oven to 180°C/Fan 160°C/Gas Mark 4. Remove the cling film, then line the pastry case with baking parchment and fill with baking beans. Blind bake for about 15 minutes or until the sides of the pastry case are lightly golden brown. Remove the baking beans and parchment, then return to the oven to bake for a further 5 minutes or until the pastry is lightly golden on the base and just cooked through. Remove from the oven and trim off the excess pastry round the rim with a sharp knife.

Brush the beaten egg yolk all over the inside of the pastry case, then return to the oven for a minute. The egg will set and form a barrier, which will help to keep the pastry crisp once it is filled with custard. Set the pastry case aside. Lower the oven temperature to 140°C/Fan 120°C/Gas Mark 1.

For the filling, pour the cream into a heavy-based pan and bring to a simmer. Meanwhile, lightly whisk the egg yolks and sugar together in a large bowl. As soon as the cream begins to bubble, take the pan off the heat. Slowly add the hot cream to the sugary yolks, stirring all the while. When fully combined, strain the mixture through a fine sieve into a jug.

Pour the custard filling into the pastry case, then generously grate nutmeg over the surface. Carefully place the tart on the bottom shelf of the oven and bake for 30–40 minutes or until the filling is set around the edges but the centre is still soft – it should have a slight wobble in the middle when the tin is gently tapped. Remove the tart from the oven and leave to cool completely. Once cold, unmould and serve sprinkled with a little more grated nutmeg, if you wish.

BAILEY'S BREAD AND BUTTER PUDDING

There is nothing like a good slug of Baileys to elevate a classic bread and butter pudding to new heights. Personally, I think bread and butter puddings should always be served warm with a generous scoop of ice cream alongside. To go with this Baileys version, I recommend a mascarpone and pecan ice cream but you won't go wrong with classic vanilla.

SERVES 8

80g unsalted butter, softened, plus extra for greasing
½ Brioche Loaf (see page 24), sliced (about 8 slices)
100g raisins
550ml double cream
175ml whole milk
8 large egg yolks
100g caster sugar
100ml Baileys Irish Cream

Preheat the oven to 180°C/Fan 160°C/ Gas Mark 4. Grease the base and sides of eight individual baking dishes or ramekins and set them on a large baking sheet. Spread the softened butter generously on the brioche slices, then cut the slices diagonally into triangles. Layer the brioche slices and raisins in the baking dishes. Set aside.

Put the cream and milk into a saucepan and bring to the boil. Whisk the egg yolks with the sugar in a large bowl. Slowly trickle the hot creamy milk over the sugary eggs, whisking constantly. Stir in the Baileys, then strain the custard mixture through a fine sieve into a jug.

Pour the custard mixture over the brioche in the dishes and leave to soak for 10 minutes. If there is any custard mixture left in the jug, pour it over the brioche now, as the slices will have soaked up some of the custard.

Bake for 30–40 minutes or until the puddings are set and golden brown on top. Leave to cool slightly before serving.

CHERRY CLAFOUTIS

Cherry clafoutis always reminds me of French summers and it is one of the simplest puddings you can make. Because it is so quick and easy to whip up, make and bake the clafoutis shortly before serving when it tastes its best.

SERVES 6

unsalted butter, softened, for
   greasing
200g cherries, pitted
4 medium egg yolks
2 medium eggs
110g caster sugar
45g plain flour
a pinch of fine sea salt
75ml double cream
sifted icing sugar, for dusting

Preheat the oven to 200°C/Fan 180°C/ Gas Mark 6. Generously butter six ramekins or individual shallow baking dishes and set them on a large baking sheet. Divide the pitted cherries among the buttered dishes.

Put the egg yolks, eggs and sugar into a large mixing bowl and whisk well together. Sift in the flour and salt and whisk until the batter is smooth. Add the cream and whisk until well incorporated. Pour the mixture over the cherries in the ramekins – they should be two-thirds full.

Bake for 10–15 minutes or until the top of each clafoutis is a light golden brown. Leave to cool slightly, then dust with icing sugar and serve whilst still warm.

CLASSICS

STICKY TOFFEE PUDDING
WITH SALTED CARAMEL

In the dead of winter, nothing beats a good sticky toffee pudding at the end of a meal. It never fails to warm my cockles, particularly when enjoyed with a glass of PX sherry or port. For me, the caramel sauce should always be salted so as to offset the intense sweetness of the pudding.

SERVES 8–10

65g unsalted butter, plus extra for
  greasing
200g pitted dried dates, roughly
  chopped
250ml water
100g soft light brown sugar
100g caster sugar
2 large eggs, at room temperature,
  lightly beaten
200g plain flour
1½ teaspoons baking powder
½ teaspoon fine sea salt
**Vanilla or Salted Caramel Ice Cream
  (see pages 175 and 186), to serve**

For the salted caramel
250ml double cream
1 teaspoon Maldon sea salt
110g liquid glucose
150g caster sugar
75g unsalted butter, diced

Preheat the oven to 180°C/Fan 160°C/Gas Mark 4. Grease a 900g loaf tin and line with baking parchment.

Put the chopped dates and water into a small saucepan and bring to the boil. Remove from the heat and leave to cool slightly, then pour the mixture into a small food processor and blend until nicely puréed. Transfer to a bowl and leave to cool completely.

Meanwhile, cream the butter with the brown and caster sugars in a large mixing bowl using an electric whisk. When the mixture is light and fluffy, gradually beat in the eggs. Sift the flour, baking powder and salt into the bowl and fold through. Finally, add the date purée and fold into the mixture until just incorporated (try not to over-mix the batter).

Pour the mixture into the greased and lined tin and bake for 30–40 minutes or until a skewer inserted into the middle comes out clean. Cool for a few minutes, then turn out the loaf on to a wire rack. Leave to cool a bit more while you make the salted caramel sauce.

To make the caramel, put the cream and salt into a heavy-based saucepan and slowly bring to a simmer, then remove from the heat. Meanwhile, put the liquid glucose into another heavy-based saucepan with 50g of the sugar. Set over medium heat and let the sugar melt slowly. Once it has, add half of the remaining sugar and let it melt slowly over medium heat. Repeat with the last of the sugar. Once all the sugar has melted, increase the heat and let the syrup cook to an amber-coloured caramel.

Take the pan off the heat and slowly stir in the hot cream. If there are any bits of hardened caramel, stir the mixture over medium heat until they have melted. Finally, stir in the butter and take the pan off the heat. (If making in advance, gently reheat the caramel before serving.)

To serve, cut the warm sticky toffee pudding into slices and place one on each serving plate. Pour the salted caramel generously over the puddings and serve immediately, with ice cream on the side, if you wish.

CHRISTMAS PUDDING

Throughout the years, I've eaten too many awful Christmas puddings that were either too stodgy, too sweet, too dry or just not up to scratch. This, on the other hand, is one of the best Christmas puddings I've made and scoffed. It is light and moist with the right amount of sweetness. Serve with simple vanilla crème anglaise (see page 240) or a good ice cream such as Vin Santo, roasted mandarin or rum and raisin, (see pages 177, 188 or 191).

MAKES FOUR 500G PUDDINGS; EACH WILL SERVE 4–6 PEOPLE

butter for greasing
225g breadcrumbs (fresh or from day-old bread)
225g suet
115g Bramley apples, peeled, cored and grated
115g carrots, peeled and grated
1 teaspoon mixed spice
30g plain flour
3 medium eggs

For the soaked fruits
225g sultanas
225g raisins
225g currants
30g candied orange peel
30g candied lemon peel
225g light brown sugar
225ml Guinness
115ml brandy

To serve
3–4 tablespoons chopped candied peel (optional)
Vanilla Crème Anglaise (see page 240), Vin Santo Ice Cream (see page 177), Roasted Mandarin Ice Cream (see page 188) or Rum and Raisin Ice Cream (see page 191),

Put all the dried fruits, candied peel and sugar into a large bowl and pour over the Guinness and brandy. Cover the bowl tightly with cling film and leave the fruits to macerate overnight.

The next day, find a pan that is large enough to fit four 500g heatproof plastic pudding moulds for steaming. Bring a kettle of water to the boil. Generously butter the pudding moulds and their matching lids.

Put the breadcrumbs, suet, apples, carrots, mixed spice and flour in a large mixing bowl and stir together. Make a well in the centre. Lightly beat the eggs and pour into the well. Add the soaked fruits with any soaking alcohol left in the bowl and fold together until the mixture is well combined. It should be quite wet. If your mixture appears a little dry, add a little splash of brandy and fold through.

Divide the mixture among the prepared pudding moulds. Level the tops, then cover with the buttered lids. To make sure that the moulds are watertight, cover each one tightly with cling film. Lower the pudding moulds into the pan, then pour in enough boiling water to come halfway up the sides of the moulds. Cover the pan with a lid and steam over medium heat for 5 hours, making sure to check the water level in the pan from time to time (you may need to top up with more boiling water from the kettle).

When the time is up, carefully lift the pudding moulds out of the pan and leave them to cool completely, still covered. Then remove all the cling film and keep the puddings in a cool, dry place until you want to serve them.

To serve each pudding, reheat by steaming for 2 hours. Take off the lid and turn out on to a cake plate. Garnish the top of the pudding with a spoonful of chopped candied peel, then flame with brandy or vodka, if you wish. Serve immediately, with crème anglaise or ice cream.

CLASSICS

SOCIAL SWEETS

PBJ MACARONS

Macarons have been all the rage for quite a while now and it is not hard to see why. When made well, they are superb and they attest to the creativity of the pastry chef. However, do not feel daunted to try and make them yourself. When you do, bear in mind the humidity level in your kitchen. Too much humidity and it will take a long time for the macarons to form their skins, which in turn, will determine the final look of the macarons. You can sandwich the macaron shells with a simple chocolate ganache but this peanut butter and cherry jam version (inspired by my signature PBJ dessert) is a delicious one.

MAKES 30–40 MACARONS

For the macaron shells
110g ground almonds
175g icing sugar
90g egg whites (about 3 medium)
45g caster sugar
30g salted roasted peanuts, finely
    chopped

For the peanut butter filling
75g smooth peanut butter
75g unsalted butter
75g icing sugar, sifted

To finish
150g Cherry Jam (see page 245)

Line two large baking sheets with silicone mats or baking parchment. (If using baking parchment, you may want to draw rows of 3cm circles to use as a size guide when piping the macarons. Flip the baking parchment over before laying it on the baking sheets so that the macarons won't have contact with the pencil marks.)

Put the ground almonds and icing sugar into the bowl of a food processor and pulse until the mixture is very finely ground and evenly combined. Take care not to overprocess the almonds – they will begin to release their oils if overheated. Sift the mixture into a large mixing bowl; discard any bits left in the sieve. Set aside.

Put the egg whites into the bowl of an electric mixer fitted with the whisk attachment. Whisk the whites on medium speed until they will hold medium peaks, then gradually add the caster sugar, a tablespoon at a time. When fully incorporated, increase the speed to high and whisk the meringue until it is stiff and glossy.

Gently fold the meringue into the dry almond mixture, just until the combined mixture will fall in a thick ribbon from the spatula and fade back into the rest of the mixture within 30 seconds. It is important not to overfold the mixture or it will be too runny.

Transfer the macaron mixture to a piping bag fitted with a 1cm plain nozzle. Pipe on to the prepared baking sheets to make 60–80 rounds about 3cm in diameter.

Sprinkle half of the macarons with a small pinch of chopped peanuts. Leave the macarons to dry out at room temperature for at least 30 minutes or until they have developed a skin on the surface.

Preheat the oven to 160°C/Fan 140°C/Gas Mark 3. Bake the macarons for 5 minutes, then turn the trays around (to ensure even cooking) and bake for a further 5–7 minutes or until the macarons are lightly golden. Remove from the oven and leave to cool on the baking sheets.

Meanwhile, prepare the peanut butter filling. Put all the ingredients into a mixing bowl and stir until well combined, then beat the mixture with an electric whisk until it is light and fluffy. Transfer to a piping bag fitted with a 5mm plain nozzle. Fill a similar piping bag with the cherry jam.

To finish the macarons, pipe a ring of peanut butter filling around the edge of the underside of the macaron shells that have peanuts on top, leaving a gap in the middle. Pipe the cherry jam into the gap, then sandwich the macarons with the remaining shells (underside to underside). It is best to leave the macarons overnight before serving, so arrange them in a suitable container, cover and keep in the fridge.

CITY SOCIAL EARL GREY TEA SOUFFLÉ

Every chef worth his salt should be able to make a good soufflé but, to be honest, it is just as achievable for the home cook. The key is to remember to properly cook out the soufflé base and let it boil for a few minutes. It is also important to have a light touch when folding the whisked egg whites into the soufflé base. The sky is the limit when it comes to flavouring a soufflé and this Earl Grey tea version from City Social is a particularly good one.

MAKES 8 INDIVIDUAL SOUFFLÉS

For the soufflé base
35g loose leaf Earl Grey tea
75ml water
315ml whole milk
65g plain flour
90g caster sugar
45g cold unsalted butter, diced, plus extra melted butter for greasing
4 medium egg yolks
finely grated dark chocolate, for the moulds
icing sugar, for dusting

For the meringue
8 medium egg whites
100g caster sugar

First, make the soufflé base. Put the Earl Grey tea and water into a saucepan and bring to the boil. Leave to boil down for a few minutes until most of the water has evaporated and you are left with 2 tablespoons of very strong tea. Pour in the milk and bring to a simmer. Simmer for 2 minutes, then strain the milky tea through a fine sieve into the measuring jug, pressing down on the tea leaves with the back of a spoon to extract as much flavour as possible. Set aside (keep the saucepan for later).

Put the flour and sugar into a large mixing bowl. Add the cold butter and rub in until the mixture resembles fine breadcrumbs. Make a well in the centre. Add the egg yolks to the well, then pour in the milky tea and mix well. Pour the mixture back into the saucepan and set over medium heat. Slowly bring to the boil, whisking constantly. The mixture will thicken as it heats. Boil for a couple of minutes, still whisking, then transfer to a wide bowl. Leave to cool, giving the mixture a stir every now and then to prevent a skin from forming. (If preparing ahead, the soufflé base can be covered and refrigerated at this stage.)

When you are ready to bake the soufflés, preheat the oven to 200°C/Fan 180°C/Gas Mark 6 and place a baking sheet on the top shelf. Generously brush the inside of eight 150ml ramekins with melted butter, using upward strokes for the sides (this will help the soufflés rise evenly). Chill the ramekins for a few minutes to set the butter, then brush with another layer of butter. Tip a little grated chocolate into each ramekin and tilt it so that it is evenly coated with chocolate. Tip out any excess.

In a large, grease-free bowl, whisk the egg whites with the sugar to make a thick, glossy meringue with firm peaks. Fold a third of the meringue into the soufflé base to loosen it, then fold in the rest of the meringue. Spoon the mixture into the prepared ramekins, filling them to the top. Give each ramekin a tap on the work surface to remove any large air bubbles. Pull a small palette knife over the surface to level it, then run the tip of the knife around the inside edge of each ramekin (this will help to release the soufflés as they rise).

Bake for 8–10 minutes or until the soufflés have fully risen – by about two-thirds of their original height – and are set on top. They should wobble slightly when moved. Dust with icing sugar and serve at once.

CLASSICS

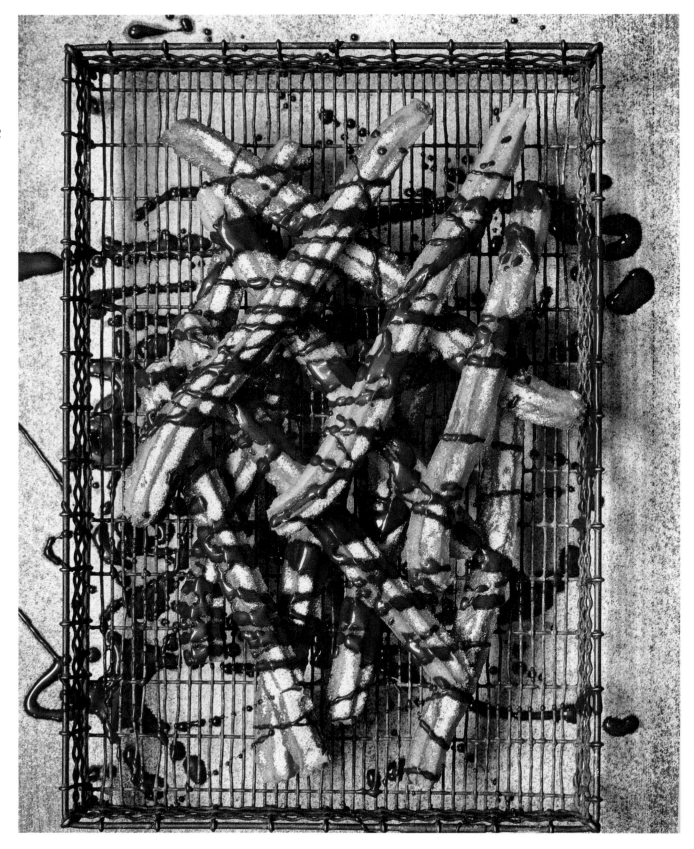

SOCIAL SWEETS

CHURROS

I can't tell you how many churros I have devoured during my time working in Spain. They were absolutely scrumptious and it was such a treat to eat them straight out of the fryer when they were still crunchy on the outside but soft inside. The obligatory chocolate sauce is simply the icing on the cake.

MAKES 30–40 CHURROS

250g plain flour
a pinch of fine sea salt
10g baking powder
40ml vegetable or groundnut oil, plus oil for deep-frying
475ml water

For the cinnamon sugar
100g caster sugar
1 tablespoon ground cinnamon

To serve (optional)
100g dark or milk chocolate, melted

Sift the flour, salt and baking powder into a large mixing bowl and make a well in the middle. Put the oil and water into a small saucepan and bring to the boil. As soon as the mixture boils, take the pan off the heat and pour the liquid into the well. Quickly mix the ingredients together using a wooden spoon or a spatula. Keep on stirring and mixing until the batter comes together and leaves the sides of the bowl. Cover the bowl with a clean kitchen towel and leave to stand for 10–15 minutes.

Meanwhile, start heating oil in a deep-fat fryer or a heavy-based pan – the oil is hot enough when it reaches 180°C (at this temperature a little batter dropped into the oil should sizzle immediately and brown in 45–60 seconds). Mix the sugar and cinnamon together in a wide bowl. Have ready a tray lined with several layers of kitchen paper.

Spoon the churros dough into a piping bag fitted with a 1.5–2cm star nozzle. Fry three to four churros at a time, to avoid crowding the pan and reducing the temperature of the oil: pipe strips of dough (about 10cm in length) directly into the oil, snipping off the ends with kitchen scissors. Deep-fry for 2 minutes on each side or until evenly golden brown and crisp. Remove with a slotted spoon and leave to drain on the paper-lined tray.

Whilst the churros are still warm, roll them in the cinnamon sugar. Then, if you like, place the churros on a wire rack set over a large tray and drizzle the melted chocolate generously over them.

SHERRY TRIFLE

A classic trifle is a showstopper, particularly when served in a gorgeous clear trifle bowl. My version is made with a generous amount of Pedro Ximénez sherry for I adore the inimitable sticky sweetness that it lends to the trifle. This recipe is also great for entertaining because you can make the lemon sponge, sherry jelly and orange and bay custard two days in advance. On the day of serving, simply top the trifle with the crème Chantilly and garnish with raspberries and grated chocolate.

SERVES 8

For the lemon sponge
65g unsalted butter, plus extra
    softened butter for greasing
65g caster sugar, plus extra 2
    tablespoons
1 large egg yolk
25g semolina
65g ground almonds
finely grated zest of ½ lemon
1 tablespoon lemon juice
1 large egg white

For the Pedro Ximénez jelly
2½ gelatine leaves
30g caster sugar
50ml water
250ml Pedro Ximénez sherry

For the orange and bay leaf custard
500ml whole milk
finely grated zest of 1 orange
6 bay leaves, torn
100g caster sugar
40g cornflour
4 large egg yolks

To assemble
150g raspberries
crème Chantilly (see page 240)
grated dark chocolate

First, make the lemon sponge. Preheat the oven to 180°C/Fan 160°C/Gas Mark 4. Grease the sides of a 15cm round cake tin and line the base with baking parchment. (If you don't have a 15cm cake tin, use the smallest cake tin you have but adjust the baking time accordingly.)

Put the butter and 65g sugar into a large mixing bowl and beat with an electric whisk until pale and fluffy. Beat in the egg yolk. Add the semolina and ground almonds followed by the lemon zest and juice. Fold the mixture together.

In another large, clean bowl, whisk the egg white with the 2 tablespoons of sugar to stiff peaks. Stir a spoonful of the meringue into the cake mixture to loosen it, then gently fold through the rest of the meringue. Pour the mixture into the prepared cake tin and level the top with a palette knife.

Bake for 20–25 minutes or until the cake is lightly golden brown and a skewer inserted into the middle comes out clean. Transfer to a wire rack to cool.

When the cake has cooled, remove it from the tin and peel off the baking parchment. Cut the cake into 2.5cm cubes. Place them in a large, glass trifle bowl. Scatter half the raspberries over the cake. Set aside while you make the sherry jelly.
Soak the gelatine leaves in a small bowl of cold water for a few minutes to soften. Meanwhile, combine the sugar and water in a small saucepan and stir over medium heat until the sugar has dissolved. Squeeze out the excess water from the gelatine leaves, then add to the pan and stir until melted. Take the pan off the heat. Stir in the sherry, then strain the mixture through a fine sieve into a jug. Pour the mixture over the cake and raspberries in the trifle bowl. Put the bowl in the fridge and leave the jelly to set for an hour or two.

To make the custard, put the milk, orange zest and bay leaves in a saucepan and bring to the boil. Remove from the heat and leave to infuse for 2 minutes. Meanwhile, combine the sugar, cornflour and egg yolks in a large bowl and whisk well together. Strain the infused milk through a fine sieve into a jug (discard the aromatics), then slowly trickle into the egg mixture, stirring constantly. Pour back into the saucepan and cook over medium heat, stirring frequently, until the mixture thickens to a thick custard. Transfer the custard to a wide bowl and leave to cool, stirring every once in a while to prevent a skin from forming. Once cooled, cover the bowl with cling film and refrigerate for an hour or two.

Lightly whisk the custard to loosen it, then spread it over the jelly layer. Chill for about 20 minutes to set the custard slightly.

To finish the trifle, spoon the crème
Chantilly evenly over the custard. Sprinkle
with grated chocolate, then finish with the
remaining raspberries. Keep in the fridge if
not serving immediately.

CLASSICS

SOCIAL SWEETS

TIRAMISU

The Italians have got it right – a good tiramisu will never go out of style! It is straightforward to make but ever so delicious. Be generous with the coffee and amaretto and you are on to a winning pudding.

SERVES 8

For the coffee syrup
300ml strong espresso
140g caster sugar
60ml Amaretto liqueur (optional)

For the mascarpone cream
120g caster sugar
50ml water
4 large egg yolks
300g mascarpone
450ml double cream

To assemble
unsalted butter for greasing
175g savoiardi or sponge finger biscuits
cocoa powder for dusting

Put the espresso and sugar into a small saucepan and bring to the boil. Remove from the heat and stir in the Amaretto. Pour the liquid into a shallow bowl and set aside.

For the mascarpone cream, put the sugar and water into a saucepan and stir over medium heat until the sugar has dissolved. Put a sugar thermometer into the pan, then increase the heat and bring the syrup to the boil. Let the syrup boil until it reaches 115°C.

Meanwhile, whisk the egg yolks in a large heatproof bowl using an electric whisk until they are pale and light. When the sugar syrup is at the right temperature, carefully trickle it into the yolks, whisking constantly. When fully incorporated, keep whisking until the egg mixture is thick and glossy and the side of the bowl no longer feels hot. Add the mascarpone and whisk to combine. Whip the cream to soft peaks in another bowl, then fold through the mascarpone mixture.

To assemble the tiramisu, lightly grease a 20 x 40cm dish. Dip half of the savoirdi or sponge finger biscuits into the coffee syrup to moisten, then arrange them on the base of the dish. Spoon over half the mascarpone cream and smooth level. Repeat with another layer of syrup-soaked biscuits and the remaining mascarpone cream. Smooth the top with a spatula or palette knife. Cover the dish with cling film and chill for a few hours or until the cream has set slightly.

Dust the top of the tiramisu with cocoa powder, then return to the fridge and chill for a few more hours, preferably overnight, before serving.

MILLEFEUILLE

A classic millefeuille consists of just two components – puff pastry and pastry cream – so needless to say it is vital to use good quality ingredients such as all butter puff pastry or better yet, homemade puff pastry. If you find it difficult to slice the millefeuille neatly, chill or freeze it for about an hour until firm, then cut it using a thin, sharp knife.

SERVES 8

500g Quick Puff Pastry (see page 238) or bought butter puff pastry
50g icing sugar, sifted, plus extra for dusting
50g unsalted butter, softened
1 quantity Crème Pâtissière (see page 240), still warm
25ml dark rum

Preheat the oven to 180°C/Fan 160°C/Gas Mark 4. On a lightly floured surface, roll out the puff pastry to a large rectangle about 3–4mm thick. Using a ruler as a guide, cut out three rectangles, each measuring 15 x 30cm. Carefully transfer the rectangles to a large baking sheet lined with a silicone mat. Dust the pastry rectangles with icing sugar, then cover with a large sheet of baking parchment. Weigh down the pastries with another heavy baking sheet placed on top.

Bake for 20 minutes, then check to see if the pastries are done: remove the top baking sheet and baking parchment. If the pastries are not golden brown and they still have grey patches of uncooked dough, turn the oven temperature down to 140°C/Fan 120°C/Gas Mark 1 and bake the pastries for a further 5–10 minutes (without the top baking sheet and parchment). Leave to cool. (If making ahead, store in airtight containers with sheets of baking parchment between the pastry layers.)

For the filling, stir the butter into the warm crème pâtissière, then leave to cool completely, stirring every once in a while to prevent a skin from forming. Once cooled, stir in the rum, then cover with cling film and keep in the fridge until needed.

When you are ready to assemble the millefeuille, lightly whisk the crème pâtissière to loosen it, then spoon into a large piping bag fitted with a 1cm round nozzle. Pipe a dot of crème pâtissière in the centre of a large serving plate, then place a puff pastry rectangle on it. Pipe a layer of crème pâtissière (using about half of it) in neat rows on top of the puff pastry. Set another puff pastry rectangle on top, then pipe a layer of the remaining crème pâtissière on this. Top with the final puff pastry rectangle and dust it with icing sugar. If you wish, trim the sides of the millefeuille to neaten. Carefully cut into eight portions to serve.

CLASSICS

STONE FRUIT CRUMBLE

I've always loved crumbles. I even go as far as to make savoury (sometimes spicy) crumbles to add texture and crunch to my starters and main courses at the restaurants. This recipe is a traditional but delightful crumble made with a mixture of plums, peaches and nectarines. It is a lovely way to use up a glut of autumnal stone fruits.

SERVES 8

butter for greasing
800g mixed stone fruits, such as
    plums, peaches and nectarines
50g caster sugar
finely grated zest of 1 orange
juice of 1 lemon
200g blackberries
Vanilla Ice Cream (see page 175) or
    Crème Anglaise (see page 240), to
    serve

For the crumble topping
100g rolled (porridge) oats
100g plain flour
125g cold unsalted butter, diced
150g light soft brown sugar
1 teaspoon ground cinnamon
1 teaspoon ground ginger
a pinch of ground cloves

Preheat the oven to 150°C/Fan 130°C/ Gas Mark 2. Generously grease a 2 litre baking dish and set aside.

Halve the fruit and remove the stones, then roughly chop into bite-sized pieces. Put the fruit into a large bowl and toss with the sugar, orange zest and lemon juice. Add the blackberries and gently toss to mix. Tip the fruit into the prepared baking dish and spread out. Warm in the oven for 15–20 minutes.

Meanwhile, prepare the crumble topping. Put the oats and flour into a wide bowl and add the diced butter. Rub the butter into the oats and flour until the mixture resembles coarse crumbs. Stir in the sugar and spices.

Remove the baking dish from the oven and spread the crumble topping evenly over the fruit. Return to the oven and bake for about 1 hour and 20 minutes or until the topping is golden brown and crisp. Serve warm, with ice cream or crème anglaise.

CARROT CAKE

Carrot cakes have a reputation for being healthy but they can be quite calorific. I cannot claim that this version is low-fat or low-sugar but it is sure to satisfy and delight. The cake will freeze well in a sealed container for up to a month. Once frosted with the white chocolate ganache, keep it refrigerated and consume within a couple of days.

MAKES A 20CM CAKE TO SERVE 8–10, OR 18 CUPCAKES

unsalted butter for greasing
2 large eggs
200g golden caster sugar
135ml grapeseed oil (or other mild/ flavourless vegetable oil)
20g apricot jam
170g peeled and grated carrots
75g drained canned pineapple, finely chopped
215g plain flour
1 teaspoon ground cinnamon
1 teaspoon bicarbonate of soda
1 teaspoon baking powder
½ teaspoon fine sea salt
70g candied orange peel, chopped
finely grated zest of 1 orange
white chocolate curls, to decorate (optional)

For the whipped white chocolate ganache
200ml whipping cream
30g liquid glucose (or equal quantities of liquid glucose and light honey)
100g white chocolate, roughly chopped

Preheat the oven to 170°C/Fan 150°C/ Gas Mark 3. Lightly grease two 20cm round springform cake tins and line with baking parchment. For cupcakes, line three 6-hole cupcake tins with paper cupcake cases.

Put the eggs and sugar into a large mixing bowl and beat with an electric whisk until the mixture is pale and light and has tripled in volume – when the whisk is lifted, the mixture falling from it should leave a ribbon trail on the surface of the mix in the bowl. Gradually whisk in the oil, then fold through the apricot jam followed by the grated carrots and chopped pineapple. Sift all the dry ingredients together into a separate bowl, then add to the whisked mixture and fold in until thoroughly incorporated. Finally, add the chopped candied peel and orange zest and fold until evenly mixed.

Divide the cake mixture between the prepared cake tins (or paper cupcake cases). Bake the cakes for 35–45 minutes, cupcakes for 20–25 minutes, or until golden brown and a skewer inserted into the middle comes out clean. Cool for a few minutes, then unmould the cakes on to a wire rack (lift the cupcakes, in their paper cases, on to a wire rack). Leave to cool completely.

For the ganache, put the cream and liquid glucose into a saucepan and slowly warm the mixture until bubbles start to appear around the edge. Meanwhile, put the chopped white chocolate into a large bowl. Pour the warm cream on to the chocolate and stir until the chocolate has melted and the mixture is smooth. Leave to cool completely, then cover with cling film and refrigerate for a couple of hours or overnight.

When ready to use, whisk the ganache to soft peaks: it should have the consistency of soft whipped cream. Sandwich the two cakes with about half the ganache, then spread or pipe the remaining ganache over the top (or pipe the ganache over the top of the cupcakes). Decorate with white chocolate curls, if you wish.

SOCIAL SWEETS

KUGELHOPF

When I was 22, I worked a season at l'Auberge de l'Ile in Lyon and it was during a trip to the Alsace that I had my first taste of kugelhopf, a soft, enriched bread similar to brioche that is studded with rum soaked raisins. This recipe makes a lightly sweetened bread but if you prefer it to be sweeter, drizzle the kugelhopf with a little vanilla syrup (see page 242) whilst it is still warm from the oven, then dust with icing sugar when it has cooled completely.

MAKES A LARGE YEAST BREAD TO SERVE 10–12

For the rum-soaked raisins
50g golden raisins
20ml dark rum

For the yeast starter
10g fresh yeast (or 7g sachet fast-action dried yeast)
35ml tepid water
50g plain flour

For the base dough
225g plain flour
40g caster sugar
1 teaspoon fine sea salt
1 medium egg, lightly beaten
125ml whole milk, at room temperature
65g unsalted butter, softened, plus extra for greasing
sifted icing sugar, for dusting

In a small bowl, soak the raisins with the rum for at least an hour but preferably overnight.

Next, if using fresh yeast, make a yeast starter. Cream the yeast with the water and leave for 10 minutes; the mixture should become foamy indicating that the yeast is activated. Add the flour and stir to mix. Cover the bowl with cling film and leave for 30–40 minutes. (If using dried yeast, you do not need to make a starter.)

To make the base dough, put the flour, sugar and salt into the bowl of an electric mixer fitted with the dough hook. (If using dried yeast, mix it in now.) Make a well in the middle of the dry ingredients and add the egg, milk, butter and yeast starter. Mix at low speed until the ingredients are well combined. The dough will be quite wet and sticky.

Turn to high speed and knead for 5–10 minutes. Add the soaked raisins and knead for a further 1–2 minutes or until the raisins are well distributed throughout the dough. Cover the bowl with cling film and leave the dough to rise in a warm spot for about an hour or until doubled in size.

Generously brush a 23cm kugelhopf mould or a bundt tin with softened butter. Knock back the risen dough by giving it a good stir with a spatula, then drop in large spoonfuls into the buttered mould to fill it evenly. Give the mould a little shake to even out the dough, then cover lightly with an oiled piece of cling film. Leave in a warm spot for 1–2 hours or until the dough has risen almost to the top of the mould.

Preheat the oven to 170°C/Fan 150°C/Gas Mark 3. Bake the kugelhopf for 30–35 minutes or until golden brown and a skewer inserted into the centre comes out clean. Leave to cool in the mould for 15 minutes, then invert the kugelhopf on to a wire rack to cool completely. Dust with icing sugar before serving. This is best enjoyed on the day of baking but will keep well for a few days if stored in a bread bin.

QUICK CHEESECAKE

It should take you less than 15–20 minutes to make this quick and easy cheesecake so it is ideal for impromptu dinner parties as well as sweltering summer days when you can't bear to turn on the oven. If you do have some time, you can prepare the cheesecake base and raspberry compote in advance, layering them into individual serving glasses to set in the refrigerator. Simply spoon over the biscuit topping when you are ready to serve.

SERVES 4–6

For the raspberry compote
250g raspberries
50g caster sugar
a twist of cracked black pepper from
    a grinder
juice of ½ lemon

For the cheesecake
250g cream cheese
90g icing sugar, sifted
½ vanilla pod, split in half, seeds
    scraped out with a knife
250ml double cream

For the crumble topping
85g digestive biscuits
15g unsalted butter, melted

First, prepare the raspberry compote. Tip the raspberries and sugar into a heavy-based saucepan and add the pepper. Gently heat the mixture, stirring initially, until the sugar dissolves and the raspberries start to break down. Remove from the heat and add the lemon juice. Transfer to a bowl and leave to cool completely. If not using soon, cover the bowl with cling film and keep in the fridge until ready to serve.

Put the cream cheese, icing sugar and vanilla seeds into a large mixing bowl. Beat the mixture together with a whisk until well combined. Whip the double cream to firm peaks in another bowl, then fold into the cheese mixture. If not using immediately, cover the bowl with cling film and keep in the fridge.

For the crumble topping, put the digestive biscuits into a clean plastic bag and crush them with a rolling pin to fine crumbs. Tip into a bowl and mix with the melted butter. (You can make this a few hours ahead, but store the crumble in an airtight container.)

To assemble the cheesecakes, spoon the cheese mixture into individual glasses or bowls. Spoon over the raspberry compote and then the crumble topping. Serve at once.

CLASSICS

BAKED CHEESECAKE

This is a rich and creamy New York-style cheesecake with a slight twist. Instead of a digestive biscuit base, I'm using a light sponge, which helps to absorb some of the moisture in the cheesecake filling. If you wish to garnish the cheesecake, try topping it with chocolate dipped strawberries, poached rhubarb, crushed pralines or peanut brittle (see page 57).

MAKES A 20CM CHEESECAKE TO SERVE 8–10

For the sponge base
50g unsalted butter, softened, plus
    extra for greasing
50g caster sugar
2 medium eggs, at room temperature,
    lightly beaten
50g plain flour
½ teaspoon baking powder

For the filling
500g full-fat cream cheese
120g caster sugar
4 large eggs, lightly beaten
65ml whipping cream
65g unsalted butter, melted and
    cooled

First, make the sponge base. Preheat the oven to 180°C/Fan 160°C/Gas Mark 4. Grease the sides of a 20cm round cake tin that is 5–6cm deep with a removable base and line the base with baking parchment.

Put the butter and sugar into a mixing bowl and beat with an electric whisk until the mixture is pale, light and fluffy. Gradually beat in the eggs, adding a tablespoon of the flour if the mixture looks like it's about to curdle. Sift the flour and baking powder together over the bowl, then fold them into the butter mixture until well combined.

Pour the sponge mixture into the prepared cake tin, spreading evenly, and level the top with a palette knife. Bake for 15–20 minutes or until the top of the sponge is lightly golden brown and a skewer inserted into the centre comes out clean. Remove from the oven and leave to cool.

Lower the oven temperature to 120°C/Fan 100°C/Gas Mark 1½. Place a large baking tin containing 3cm of water on the floor of the oven. (This creates steam in the oven, which helps to ensure that the cheesecake does not form a skin during baking.)

To make the cheesecake filling, beat the cream cheese with the sugar using an electric whisk. Gradually beat in the eggs followed by the cream. Finally, add the cooled melted butter and beat again until well combined. Pour the mixture into the cake tin over the sponge base.

Place the cheesecake on the lower shelf of the oven and bake for 1–1½ hours or until the filling is set around the edges but still wobbles slightly in the middle when gently shaken.

Remove from the oven and leave to cool completely before chilling for a couple of hours until firm. Unmould, slice and serve with fresh berries or a fruit compote.

CRÈME BRÛLÉE

Who could resist a lovely and unctuous crème brûlée with its crunchy caramelised sugar topping? This version is made with classic vanilla but you can certainly add different flavours to the custard, according to your preferences. One of my wintertime favourites is a crème brûlée topped with Armagnac-soaked prunes. In the summer, I'm partial to a lighter coconut crème brûlée served with pineapple and coconut and Malibu sorbet (see page 198).

MAKES 10 CRÈME BRÛLÉES

550ml double cream
1 vanilla pod, split in half, seeds scraped out with a knife
7 medium egg yolks
70g caster sugar, plus extra for sprinkling

Preheat the oven to 140°C/Fan 120°C/Gas Mark 1. Place ten 150ml ramekins into a deep, wide baking tray. Bring a kettle of water to the boil.

Put the cream and the vanilla pod and seeds into a heavy-based saucepan set over medium-high heat. Meanwhile, whisk together the egg yolks and sugar in a large bowl. When the cream starts steaming and bubbles appear around the edge, take the pan off the heat. Slowly pour the hot cream over the sugary eggs, stirring constantly. When all the cream has been incorporated, strain the mixture through a fine sieve into a jug.

Pour into the ramekins, dividing the mixture evenly. Add enough boiling water to the baking tray to come halfway up the sides of the ramekins. Cover the baking tray with a large piece of foil. Very carefully place the tray on the middle shelf of the oven. Bake for 25–35 minutes or until the custards are just set – they should wobble slightly in the middle when the tray is tapped.

Remove the baking tray from the oven and leave to cool before lifting the ramekins out of the tray. Pour off the water, then return the ramekins to the tray. Cover with cling film and refrigerate for a few hours.

Just before serving, sprinkle each custard with a thin, even coating of caster sugar (about 1½ teaspoons each). Run a blowtorch over the sugar, going round and round, until the sugar is evenly melted and caramelised. If you prefer, you could pop the ramekins on to a baking sheet and caramelise under a hot grill for a couple of minutes, watching closely as the sugar will melt quickly and could burn. Leave the crème brûlées to sit for a few minutes before serving.

RESTaURaNT DESSERTS

RESTAURANT DESSERTS

102/ CRÈME CATALAN 105/ CHOCOLAATE NEMESIS WITH VIN SANTO, MASCARPONE AND AMARETTO 107/ MISSISSIPPI MUD SLIDE SUNDAE 108/ PASSION FRUIT, MANGO AND CORIANDER ('FLAVOURS OF THAILAND') 111/ CINNAMON DOUGHNUTS WITH APPLE FILLING, MAPLE GLAZE AND VANILLA CRÈME ANGLAISE 113/ MILK CHOCOLATE CREMEUX, LOVAGE ICE CREAM, COCOA NIBS AND HAZELNUTS 114/ CHOCOLATE MOUSSE, CHOCOLATE SOIL, BLACKBERRY GEL AND VANILLA CHURROS 117/ CHAMPAGNE-POACHED PEACHES WITH VANILLA YOGHURT TERRINE

118/ LEMON MERINGUE PIE WITH LEMONADE PARFAIT, BLACK PEPPER PASTRY AND SOUR YOGHURT 121/ BASIL SORBET, STRAWBERRIES, YUZU YOGHURT AND BLACK PEPPER MERINGUE 122/ CHOCOLATE AND STRAWBERRY ÉCLAIR WITH CHOCOLATE SORBET 124/ 'WAGON WHEEL' TOASTED MARSHMALLOW, SALTED CARAMEL, RASPBERRY AND CHOCOLATE 127/ PEACHES WITH RASPBERRY, GRANOLA AND PUFF PASTRY ICE CREAM 128/ ENGLISH STRAWBERRY BAKEWELL WITH AMARETTO AND HIBISCUS 131/ BREAD AND BUTTER PUDDING WITH VANILLA AND PECAN ICE CREAM 132/ GREEN TEA CAKE, YUZU AND RASPBERRIES

135/ RED DOT BREWHOUSE SAUVIGNON ALE, YEAST, HOPS, COCOA PRETZEL AND APRICOTS 137/ MATCHA, STRAWBERRY, SOUR PLUM AND TAHINI CREAM ('MATCHA') 141/ TOASTED COCONUT CRÈME BRÛLÉE WITH PINEAPPLE, COCONUT AND MALIBU SORBET 142/ CRISPY LEMON MERINGUE, CUCUMBER SORBET AND GIN GEL 145/ COFFEE AND MANDARIN ('MANDARIN') 149/ CHOCOLATE MOUSSE, HAZELNUT & BURNT ORANGE 150/ SCOTTISH RASPBERRY PAVLOVA WITH VANILLA CREAM AND RED WINE AND RASPBERRY GRANITA

153/ COCONUT MERINGUE WITH MANGO SORBET, PINEAPPLE, COCONUT AND CURRY CRUMBLE 157/ APPLE, BEETROOT AND CARROT ('ABC') 158/ COCONUT PANNA COTTA, MANGO SORBET, RAW PEACH SALAD, CANDIED TARRAGON AND ORANGE BISCUIT 161/ CHOCOLATE GANACHE WITH SEA SALT AND PISTACHIO PARFAIT 162/ PEANUT PARFAIT, RED FRUIT AND SALTED PEANUT CARAMEL 165/ GOAT'S CHEESE, FROMAGE FRAIS SORBET, HONEYCOMB AND SWEET WALNUTS 166/ HOT CHOCOLATE MOELLEUX WITH SEA SALT AND ALMOND ICE CREAM

CRÈME CATALAN

Crème Catalan is such a perfect Spanish dessert that I find no need to modify the flavour and texture of the pudding. The only thing I've done differently here is to add a little gelatine to the crème so that when set, it can be spooned neatly onto individual serving plates. At the restaurants, we serve our crème Catalan with almond croquants and dehydrated black olives to add texture to the dessert, but you can opt to simply serve the custards with fresh berries and mint leaves.

SERVES 6

For the crème Catalan
600ml whole milk
finely grated zest of 1 small lemon
2 cinnamon sticks
2 gelatine leaves
4 large egg yolks
120g caster sugar
1 teaspoon cornflour

For the caramel almond croquant
100g liquid glucose
100g caster sugar
100ml water
50g flaked almonds

For the dehydrated black olives
100g pitted black olives

To serve
Raspberry Jam (see page 245)
250–300g fresh strawberries and
    raspberries
a handful of baby mint leaves
    (optional)

To make the crème Catalan, put the milk, lemon zest and cinnamon sticks into a heavy-based saucepan and slowly bring to a simmer. Soak the gelatine leaves in a small bowl of cold water to soften.

Stir together the egg yolks, sugar and cornflour in large heatproof bowl. When the milk begins to simmer, take the pan off the heat and remove the cinnamon sticks, then slowly trickle the hot milk on to the yolk mixture, stirring constantly. Set the bowl over a pan of gently simmering water and stir with a wooden spoon for a few minutes until the mixture thickens to a light custard that will coat the back of the spoon.

Squeeze excess water out of the gelatine leaves, then add them to the custard and stir until melted. Take the bowl off the pan and continue to stir until the custard has cooled a little. Strain the custard through a fine sieve into a wide bowl. Place a sheet of cling film on top of the custard to prevent a skin from forming. Leave to cool completely, then chill for a few hours until set.

For the caramel almond croquant, line two large baking sheets with silicone mat. Put the liquid glucose, sugar and water into a heavy-based pan and stir over medium heat until the sugar and glucose have dissolved. Increase the heat to high and let the syrup boil for few minutes until it begins to caramelise. When the sugar syrup has turned an amber colour, take the pan off the heat and tip in the almonds. Quickly stir to coat the almonds in the syrup, then spread the mixture thinly on one of the lined baking sheets. The caramel will set as it cools.

Once the caramel croquant is hard and brittle, preheat the oven to 160°C/Fan 140°C/Gas Mark 3. Break the caramel into small pieces and place in a food processor. Grind to a fine powder. Spread the powder thinly on the two baking sheets. (If you like, use a stencil to create decorative shapes for the croquant.) Bake for 10–15 minutes or until melted and lightly caramelised. Leave to cool completely before storing between sheets of silicone paper in an airtight container.

For the dehydrated olives, turn the oven to the lowest setting, about 100°C/Fan 80°C/Gas Mark ¼. Spread out the olives on a baking tray and dry out for 1–1½ hours or until they are crisp (eat one to check that it is completely dried out). Cool, then finely chop the olives. Store in an airtight container until ready to use (the olives will keep for a few months).

To assemble the dessert, place one large or several small spoonfuls of crème Catalan in each wide serving bowl. Spoon or pipe little mounds of raspberry jam around the bowl. Hull the strawberries and cut any larger ones in half or into quarters, then add these and the raspberries to the bowl. Garnish with caramel croquant and scatter over some dehydrated black olives. Serve at once.

RESTAURANT DESSERTS

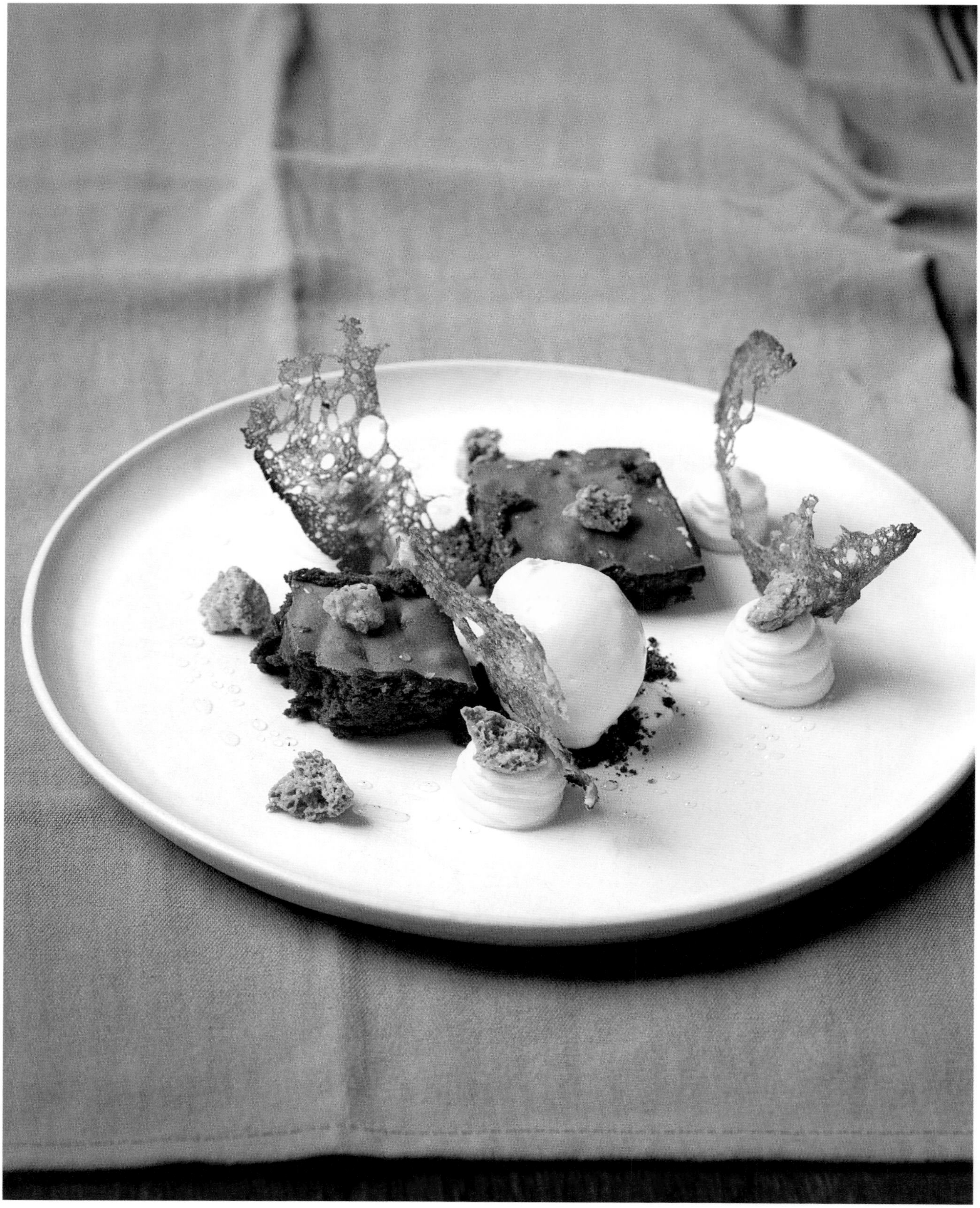

CHOCOLATE NEMESIS WITH VIN SANTO, MASCARPONE AND AMARETTO

This is a homage to the amazing chocolate nemesis made famous by Ruth Rogers and Rose Grey at the River Café in the mid-nineties. The River Café serves their chocolate nemesis simply with some crème fraîche and seasonal berries but I have vamped up the dessert with wonderful Italian ingredients such as Vin Santo, coffee, mascarpone and amaretto. A must try for any chocolate lover!

SERVES 8

For the amaretti biscuits (makes about 24)
70g blanched (skinned) hazelnuts
200g caster sugar
a pinch of fine sea salt
125g ground almonds
2 medium egg whites
40ml Amaretto liqueur
icing sugar, for dusting

For the Chocolate Nemesis
110g unsalted butter, diced, plus extra for greasing
185g dark chocolate (with about 70% cocoa solids), chopped
3 medium eggs
185g caster sugar

For the coffee toasts
½ loaf of white sourdough (about 150g)
1½ teaspoons good-quality instant coffee
25g caster sugar
150ml boiling water
olive oil, for drizzling

For the Amaretto cream
250g mascarpone
30ml Amaretto liqueur
35g caster or icing sugar

To serve
Chocolate Soil (see page 242)
Vin Santo Ice Cream (see page 177)

First make the amaretti biscuits. Preheat the oven to 180°C/Fan 160°C/Gas Mark 4. Spread out the hazelnuts in a single layer on a rimmed baking sheet. Toast in the oven for 10–15 minutes, stirring every 5 minutes or so, until they are lightly golden. Leave to cool.

Line two large baking sheets with silicone mats or lightly greased sheets of baking parchment. Put the cooled hazelnuts into a food processor, add the sugar and salt, and blitz until the nuts are finely ground (take care not to over-process the nuts or they will begin to release their oil and become pasty). Tip the ground hazelnuts into a large mixing bowl and mix in the ground almonds. In another bowl, whisk the egg whites to stiff peaks, then fold through the Amaretto. Add to the nut mixture and fold in until evenly combined.

You can either drop teaspoonfuls of the mixture on to the baking sheets or pipe neat 5cm rounds using a piping bag fitted with a plain 1cm wide nozzle. Do make sure to space the rounds about 2.5cm apart as they will expand during baking. Dust them generously with sifted icing sugar, then leave to rest for about 20 minutes at room temperature.

Preheat the oven to 170°C/Fan 150°C/ Gas Mark 2. Bake the amaretti for 15–20 minutes or until they are golden brown and crisp. Leave to cool on the baking sheets for a few minutes, then transfer to a wire rack to cool completely. Keep in an airtight container until ready to serve. Leave the oven on at the same temperature if you are going to make the Chocolate Nemesis straight away.

For the Chocolate Nemesis, grease a 20cm square cake tin and line with baking parchment, then set it in a large roasting tin. Put the butter and chocolate into a heatproof bowl, set over a pan of gently simmering water and stir until the chocolate and butter have melted and the mixture is smooth. Remove the bowl from the pan and leave to cool.

Meanwhile, beat the eggs and sugar together with an electric whisk until the mixture is pale, fluffy and tripled in volume. Gently fold the whisked eggs through the chocolate mixture until just combined. Pour the mixture into the prepared cake tin (set in the roasting tin) and level the top with a spatula.

Pull out the middle shelf of the oven slightly and set the roasting tin on it. Pour hot water into the roasting tin to come two-thirds up the sides of the cake tin. Gently push the oven shelf back into the oven, then bake the cake for 35–45 minutes or until set (test by gently pressing in the centre with a fingertip: the cake should spring back). Remove the cake tin from the roasting tin of water and leave to cool

(continued on page 106)

completely before unmoulding. Cut into
16 pieces (about 5cm square) and keep in a
cake tin at room temperature.

To make the coffee toasts, freeze the
sourdough for about 30 minutes (to make
it easier to slice). Preheat the oven to
140°C/Fan 120°C/Gas Mark 1. Slice the
sourdough as thinly as possible (it doesn't
matter if the slices do not have neat edges,
but the thinner they are the better). Lay
them on a large baking sheet lined with
a silicone mat or baking parchment. Put
the coffee, sugar and boiling water into a
jug and stir until the sugar and coffee have
dissolved. Brush the coffee mixture over
the bread slices, then drizzle a little olive oil
over them. Bake for 30 minutes, then turn
the slices over and bake for a further 15–25
minutes or until the toasts are completely
dry and crisp. Leave to cool before storing
in an airtight container. To use, break into
smaller pieces.

For the Amaretto cream, stir all the
ingredients together in a bowl until the
sugar has dissolved and the cream is thick.
Spoon the cream into a piping bag fitted
with a 4–5mm plain nozzle. Secure the bag
and keep in the fridge until ready to serve.

To assemble the dessert, place a couple
of Chocolate Nemesis squares on each
serving plate. Add a neat pile of chocolate
soil alongside, then pipe 3 little mounds of
Amaretto cream around the plate. Crumble
some amaretti biscuits over the plate, then
stick a piece of coffee toast on each mound
of Amaretto cream. Finally, add a neat
scoop or quenelle of ice cream on top of
the chocolate soil and serve at once.

MISSISSIPPI MUD SLIDE SUNDAE

I am a big fan of traditional ice cream parlours, so much so that on our dessert menu at the Social Eating House we have a section dedicated to ice cream sundaes. Just as you would find in any old-style ice cream parlour, our ice creams are served in vintage sundae glasses, which provide a touch of nostalgia. The Mississippi Mud Pie is a perennially popular sundae and we've had it on our menu for a long while. Our guests particularly love the combination of chocolate, rum and coffee. Saying that, do treat this recipe as a rough guide and layer your sundae with as many (or as few) flavours as you wish.

SERVES 8

Chocolate Brownie (see page 44), cut into 1cm cubes

For the rum caramel
250g caster sugar
175ml double cream
25g unsalted butter
scant ½ teaspoon fine sea salt
50ml dark rum

For the coffee and vanilla cream
500ml double cream
35g caster sugar
2 tablespoons instant coffee granules
1 vanilla pod, split in half, seeds scraped out with a knife

To serve
Chocolate Ice Cream (see page 190)
Rum and Raisin Ice Cream (see page 191)
Chocolate Soil (see page 242)

To make the rum caramel, tip the sugar into a heavy-based pan and set over medium-high heat. Gently warm the cream in another smaller saucepan. As the sugar begins to melt around the edges, tilt the pan from side to side to encourage the sugar to melt evenly, then boil until it turns to an amber-coloured caramel. Immediately take the pan off the heat and carefully pour in the warm cream, standing back as the hot caramel will spit and splutter. Swirl the caramel to mix it with the cream. Should any bits of caramel harden upon contact with the cream, return the pan to a medium heat and stir until the mixture is smooth. Add the butter, salt and rum and stir until the butter has melted. Let the rum caramel cool completely, then pour it into a squeezy bottle, ready for serving.

To make the coffee and vanilla cream, pour 100ml of the cream into a small heavy-based saucepan and add the sugar, coffee granules and vanilla pod and seeds. Set the pan on a medium heat and stir until the sugar and coffee have dissolved. Strain the mixture through a fine sieve into a large mixing bowl and leave to cool completely, giving the mixture a stir every once in a while to prevent a skin from forming.

Once the coffee and vanilla cream has cooled, add the remaining cream and whip the mixture to medium peaks using an electric whisk. Cover with cling film and chill for a few hours. When ready to serve, spoon the whipped cream into one or two piping bags fitted with large 1–2cm fluted nozzles.

To assemble each dessert, pipe a little coffee and vanilla cream into the base of a tall ice-cream sundae glass. Add a scoop of chocolate ice cream followed by a few cubes of chocolate brownie. Drizzle in a little rum caramel, then add a scoop of rum and raisin ice cream. Pipe a final layer of coffee and vanilla cream over this. Arrange a handful of brownie cubes around the cream and add a teaspoonful of chocolate soil on top. Finally, drizzle over a little more rum caramel and serve at once.

PASSION FRUIT, MANGO AND CORIANDER ('FLAVOURS OF THAILAND')

Ever since I worked with Stephen Terry at Coast, I've been a fan of incorporating Thai flavours in my desserts, and this deconstructed cheesecake is simply sublime. The coriander glass is optional, but you do need the fresh mango and coriander to offset the richness of the passion fruit mousse and shaved shortbread. Isomalt can be ordered from specialist online grocers.

SERVES 8–10

For the passion fruit cheesecake mousse
90ml strained passion fruit juice
60g icing sugar
5g powdered gelatine
100ml double cream
1 medium egg
4 medium egg yolks
150g full-fat cream cheese

For the shaved shortbread
80g unsalted butter, softened, plus 75g melted unsalted butter
2g sea salt
35g soft light brown sugar
50g ground almonds
75g plain flour
50g white chocolate, melted

For the mango and lemongrass jelly
280g chopped mango flesh
2 lemongrass stalks, chopped
200ml water
60g caster sugar
16g powdered gelatine

For the coriander glass
100g isomalt sugar
100g liquid glucose
3g dried coriander leaves

To assemble
diced fresh mango
a handful of coriander shoots (or baby coriander leaves)
Vanilla Stock Syrup (see page 242), for drizzling
1 kaffir lime, frozen

Start with the cheesecake. Put the passion fruit juice and icing sugar into a small saucepan and sprinkle over the powdered gelatine. Leave the gelatine to 'sponge' for a minute or two, then warm the mixture over medium heat, stirring until the gelatine and sugar have dissolved. Take the pan off the heat and set aside.

In a large heatproof bowl, whisk together the double cream, egg and egg yolks using an electric whisk. Set the bowl over a pan of gently simmering water and whisk the mixture until it thickens. Take the bowl off the pan, then add the passion fruit mixture and the cream cheese. Whisk until smooth. Pour the mixture into a bowl, cover with cling film and chill overnight.

The next day, whisk the set passion fruit mixture until it has the consistency of a mousse. Spoon it into a large piping bag fitted with a 1cm plain nozzle. Keep in the fridge until ready to serve.

To make the shaved shortbread, preheat the oven to 160°C/Fan 140°C/Gas Mark 3. Line a baking sheet with a silicone mat. In a large mixing bowl, beat the softened butter with the salt and sugar until the mixture is pale and light in texture. Sift in the ground almonds and flour and fold through. Add the melted chocolate and fold into the dough until evenly mixed.

Scrape the shortbread dough on to the silicone mat and roughly shape it into a rectangle. Lay a sheet of baking parchment over the dough and roll it out to a large rectangle the thickness of a £1 coin. Remove the parchment, then bake the shortbread for 12–14 minutes or until the edges are lightly golden but not too brown. Leave to cool on the baking sheet. Once cold, break the shortbread into pieces and place in a food processor. With the motor running, slowly pour in the melted butter. Scrape the buttery shortbread mixture on to a large piece of cling film and press it into the shape of a log. Wrap well and freeze for at least an hour or until firm.

For the mango and lemongrass jelly, blend the mango flesh to a smooth purée in a food processor. Transfer to a bowl and set aside. Put the chopped lemongrass, water and sugar in a saucepan and stir over medium heat until the sugar has dissolved. B zoil for 2 minutes. Meanwhile, put a tablespoon of water into a small bowl and sprinkle the gelatine over it, then leave to 'sponge' for a minute or two. Add the gelatine to the hot lemongrass syrup along with the mango purée and stir, then take the pan off the heat and leave to cool slightly. Strain the mixture through a fine sieve into a shallow container, or into a small baking tray. Cover and chill for a few hours or until set. Before serving, cut the jelly into small cubes.

To make the coriander glass, put the isomalt and liquid glucose into a heavy-based saucepan and place over medium heat. Place a sugar thermometer in the pan and bring to the boil. Meanwhile, line a baking tray with a silicone mat. When the syrup is boiling, let it boil until it reaches 160°C, then remove from the heat and leave to cool down to 135°C. While the syrup is cooling, grind the coriander leaves to a powder using a coffee or spice mill. Tip this powder into the pan and quickly mix with the syrup. Immediately pour the mixture on to the silicone mat, then leave to cool. It will become hard and brittle. Once set, carefully lift the coriander glass from the silicone mat and break into 8–10 large pieces. Keep between sheets of baking parchment in an airtight container until ready to serve.

When you are ready to assemble the dessert, take shavings from the frozen shortbread log with a cheese grater (or a vegetable peeler). Place a neat pile of shortbread shavings on each serving plate. Pipe the cheesecake mousse over the shavings, then arrange diced mango and cubes of mango and lemongrass jelly on the mousse and around the plate. Top each serving with a piece of coriander glass, then garnish with coriander shoots. Drizzle a little vanilla syrup around the plates and finish with a bit of finely grated kaffir lime zest. Serve immediately.

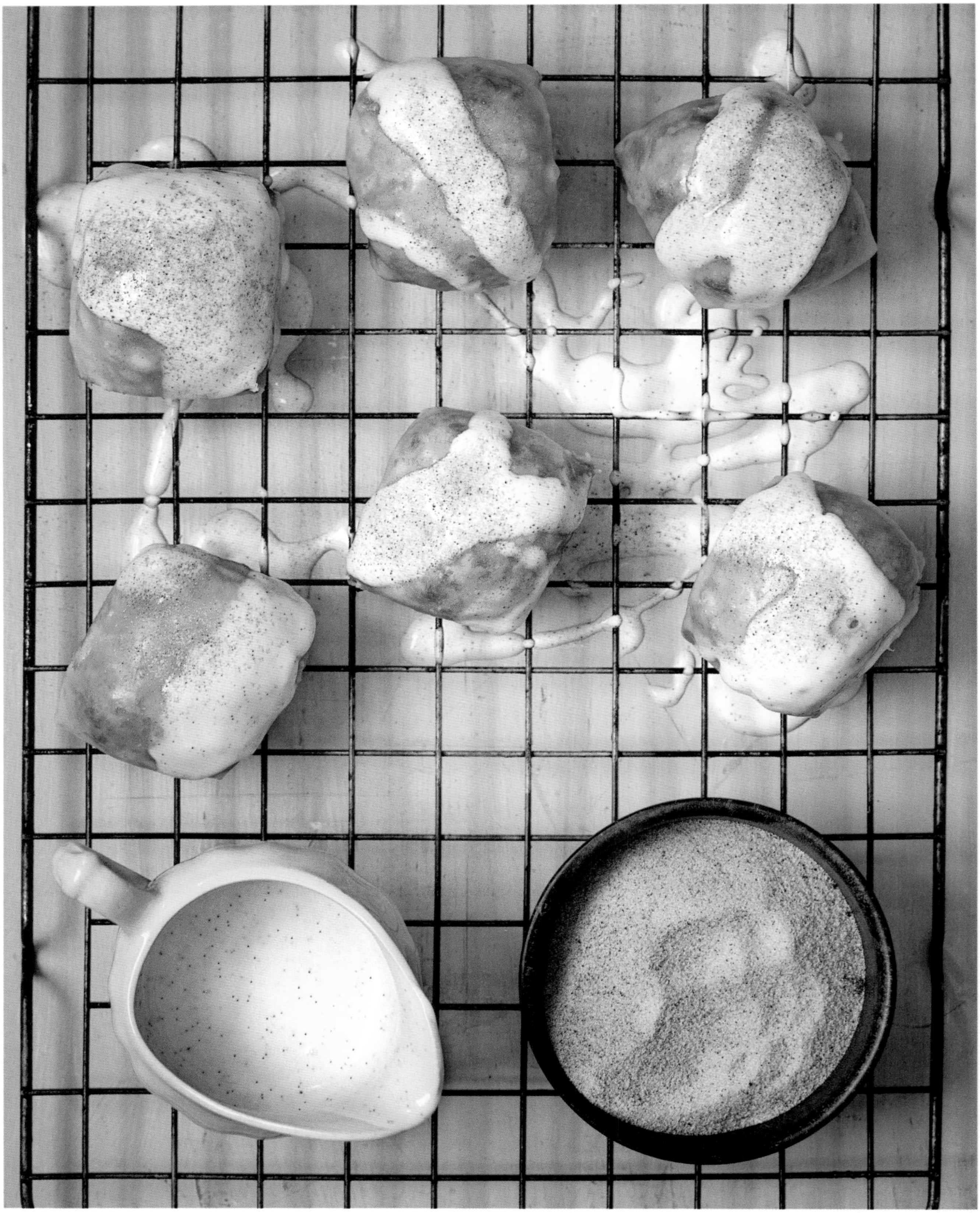

CINNAMON DOUGHNUTS WITH APPLE FILLING, MAPLE GLAZE AND VANILLA CRÈME ANGLAISE

Everyone loves a great doughnut and this is one of the best recipes I've tried. Here, soft, pillowy cinnamon doughnuts are stuffed with a lovely and moist apple filling and then coated with a beautiful maple glaze. At Little Social, our doughnuts are accompanied by little jugs of crème anglaise for the ultimate indulgence. They may be rich and calorific but they are certainly worth every bite.

MAKES ABOUT 30 DOUGHNUTS TO SERVE 10

For the doughnuts
350g plain flour
40g caster sugar
2 teaspoons fine sea salt
20g fresh yeast (or 10g fast-action dried yeast)
140ml tepid whole milk
5 large egg yolks
90g unsalted butter, softened
groundnut or vegetable oil, for deep-frying

For the apple filling
juice of ½ lemon
750g Bramley apples
225g caster sugar
25g unsalted butter

For the maple glaze
20ml maple syrup
1 tablespoon water
100g icing sugar, sifted

For the cinnamon sugar
100g caster sugar
1 teaspoon ground cinnamon

To serve
double recipe quantity of Vanilla Crème Anglaise (see page 240)

First make the doughnuts. Put the flour, sugar and salt into the bowl of an electric mixer fitted with the dough hook. (If using dried yeast, add it to the bowl now.) Stir to mix, then make a well in the middle. In a small bowl, stir the fresh yeast with a little milk until creamy, then set aside for a few minutes until foamy. Add to the well in the flour along with the egg yolks and remaining milk. Mix on low speed to combine, then increase the speed slightly and continue to mix until a dough forms.

Reduce the speed a little before adding the butter, a little at a time, and continue mixing until it is fully incorporated. If the dough seems too wet, mix in a little more flour, a tablespoonful at a time. Increase the speed and knead the dough for a couple of minutes until it is smooth and elastic. Cover the bowl with cling film and leave the dough to rise in a warm spot for 1–2 hours or until doubled in size.

Meanwhile, make the apple filling. Have ready a bowl of water and add the lemon juice to it. Peel, core and roughly chop the apples. As you chop them, immediately put them into the bowl of acidulated water to prevent them from browning. Drain the apples and pat dry with a kitchen towel, then tip into a heavy-based pan and add the sugar and butter. Cook over low heat, stirring occasionally, for about 30 minutes or until the apples are very soft. If there seems to be too much liquid, continue to cook over low heat until the mixture has thickened. Transfer the stewed apples to a food

processor and blitz until smooth, stopping the machine to scrape down the sides once or twice. Pass the apple purée through a sieve into a bowl and leave to cool completely, then spoon into a plastic squeezy bottle with a long tip (or a piping bag fitted with a long, thin nozzle). Set aside.

Knock back the risen dough and lightly knead it on a floured surface. Roll out the dough to a 1cm-thick square or rectangular shape. Line two baking sheets with baking parchment or silicone mats. Place the dough on one of the baking sheets and chill in the freezer for about 30 minutes or until the dough is semi-frozen (this will make it easier to cut).

Use a sharp knife to cut the dough into 4cm squares. Arrange them, spaced slightly apart, on the lined baking sheets. Cover with lightly greased cling film and leave in a warm spot for about an hour or until the dough squares are one-and-a-half times their original size.

For the maple glaze, combine all the ingredients in a bowl and whisk until smooth. If the glaze seems too thick, add a little more water, a tiny splash at a time, and stir well until you get the desired consistency. Conversely, if the glaze is too thin, stir in more icing sugar.

Mix the caster sugar and cinnamon together on a plate.

Heat 4–5cm of oil in a deep, heavy pan (or a deep-fat fryer) to 170°C. Deep-fry the doughnuts, in small batches, for about

(continued on page 112)

2 minutes or until golden brown all over. Remove with a slotted spoon and drain on a tray lined with several layers of kitchen paper. While the doughnuts are still warm, pipe the apple filling into the centre of each, then roll in the cinnamon sugar.

Once all the doughnuts have been deep-fried, filled and sugared, glaze them in several batches. Place a few in a single layer on a wire rack set over a large baking tray. Drizzle the maple glaze over them and leave to set slightly before transferring them to a serving plate. Serve warm or at room temperature with vanilla crème anglaise.

MILK CHOCOLATE CREMEUX, LOVAGE ICE CREAM, COCOA NIBS AND HAZELNUTS

'Cremeux' is French for creamy and this rich, dense and opulent chocolate mousse is ideal paired with lovage ice cream, slightly bitter cocoa nibs and crunchy hazelnuts for an interesting contrast of flavours and textures. A Mediterranean herb that was popular in old English gardens, lovage has now lost pride of place to the ubiquitous parsley. Some say its flavour is similar to a cross between parsley and celery. If you can't find it, try using celery leaves and seeds or other herbs such as parsley or thyme.

SERVES 10

For the milk chocolate cremeux
700g milk chocolate (with 40% cocoa solids), roughly chopped
250ml double cream
250ml whole milk
10 large egg yolks
100g caster sugar

For the white balsamic syrup
120ml water
200g caster sugar
95g liquid glucose
100ml white balsamic vinegar

For the cocoa nib and hazelnut tuiles
125g caster sugar
50g toasted hazelnuts, roughly chopped
a pinch of fine sea salt
20g roasted cocoa nibs (grué de cacao)

To serve
a few handfuls of toasted hazelnuts, lightly crushed

a few handfuls of roasted cocoa nibs (grué de cacao)
Lovage Ice Cream (see page 189)

To make the milk chocolate cremeux, put the chocolate in a heatproof bowl, set the bowl over a pan of gently simmering water and stir occasionally until the chocolate has melted. Take the bowl off the pan and set aside.

Put the cream and milk into a heavy-based saucepan and set it over medium heat. In a large mixing bowl, whisk together the egg yolks and sugar. When the creamy milk begins to steam and bubbles start to form around the edge, slowly trickle on to the sugary yolks, whisking constantly. When fully incorporated, pour the mixture back into the pan and stir with a wooden spoon over medium-low heat until thickened to a light custard that will just coat the spoon. Leave to cool slightly until the custard is about the same temperature as the melted chocolate, then slowly add the custard to the chocolate, stirring gently. Cover the bowl with cling film and keep in the fridge until ready to serve.

For the balsamic syrup, put the water, sugar and liquid glucose into a heavy-based saucepan and stir over a gentle heat until the sugar has dissolved. Increase the heat and bring the syrup to the boil. Boil for about a minute, then take the pan off the heat and stir in the vinegar. Leave to cool completely before pouring the syrup into a small squeezy bottle or jar. Cover and keep in the fridge until ready to serve.

For the cocoa nib and hazelnut tuiles, line a baking sheet with a silicone mat.

Put the sugar and a small splash of water into a heavy-based pan and stir over low heat until the sugar has dissolved. Increase the heat to high and let the syrup boil vigorously until it turns to an amber-coloured caramel. Take the pan off the heat and immediately tip in the chopped hazelnuts and salt. Quickly stir in the hazelnuts to coat them evenly with the caramel, then tip the mixture on to the lined baking sheet. The caramel will harden to a praline as it cools.

Preheat the oven to 150°C/Fan 130°C/ Gas Mark 2. Break the hazelnut praline into small pieces and grind in a food processor to fine crumbs. Tip on to the silicone-lined baking sheet and spread out evenly. Sprinkle over the cocoa nibs. Bake for 10–15 minutes or until the praline has melted to a light golden brown sheet. Leave to cool completely. Once set and hard, break into shards. Keep in an airtight container until ready to serve.

Half an hour before you are ready to serve, take the milk chocolate cremeux out of the fridge. Lightly whisk the mixture to loosen it, then spoon into a large piping bag fitted with a 1cm plain nozzle.

To assemble the dessert, put a small handful of crushed hazelnuts and cocoa nibs in the centre of each serving plate. Pipe three mounds of chocolate cremeux around the plate, then place a neat scoop or quenelle of ice cream in the middle, on top of the crushed hazelnut mixture. Drizzle balsamic syrup around the plate and garnish with the shards of hazelnut tuile. Serve immediately.

CHOCOLATE MOUSSE, CHOCOLATE SOIL, BLACKBERRY GEL AND VANILLA CHURROS

This is another way to serve the delicious chocolate mousse on page 149 but this time, I'm serving it with a lovely blackberry gel and mini vanilla churros. I became addicted to churros after spending time in Spain so they feature quite often in my recipes. Here, the churros are made into tiny bites to serve as a garnish for the chocolate mousse and it is a fun way to incorporate them into a fancy dessert.

SERVES 8–10

1 quantity Chocolate Mousse (see
   page 149)

For the blackberry gel
400g blackberries
40g caster sugar
5g powdered pectin

For the vanilla churros
165ml whole milk
50g unsalted butter
10g caster sugar
¼ teaspoon sea salt
½ vanilla pod, split in half, seeds
   scraped out with a knife
100g plain flour
1 large egg
1 large egg yolk
groundnut or other flavourless
   vegetable oil, for deep-frying

For the cinnamon sugar
50g caster sugar
1½ teaspoons ground cinnamon

To serve
Chocolate Soil (see page 242)

Make the chocolate mousse mixture and spoon it into individual serving glasses; they should be no more than three-quarters full. Refrigerate the mousse for a few hours, or overnight, to set.

For the blackberry gel, put the blackberries into a saucepan and set over medium-high heat. Mash the blackberries with a potato masher and cook for a few minutes until they are very soft. Pass the berries through a sieve into a clean pan, pressing down on the pulp with a ladle or spatula to extract as much blackberry juice and purée as possible.

Put the pan of blackberry juice on high heat and bring to the boil. Mix together the sugar and pectin, then add to the pan. Stir until the sugar has dissolved and the mixture thickened. Take the pan off the heat and leave to cool slightly before spooning a generous layer of blackberry gel over each chocolate mousse. Return to the fridge to set.

To make the vanilla churros, put the milk, butter, sugar, salt and vanilla seeds into a saucepan and set it over medium heat. Give the mixture a stir. Once the sugar has dissolved and the butter melted, increase the heat and bring the mixture to the boil. Meanwhile, sift the flour twice. When the mixture comes to a rolling boil, tip in the sifted flour and quickly stir to combine the ingredients. Keep stirring until the mixture comes together into a dough that pulls away from the side of the pan. Transfer the dough to a large mixing bowl and beat it a little. Leave to cool.

Lightly beat the egg and yolk together in a small bowl, then gradually add to the dough, beating well between each addition until the mixture is smooth. Spoon the dough into a large piping bag fitted with a 1cm star tip nozzle.

Heat 5–6cm of oil in a deep pan (or a deep-fat fryer) to 180°C. Have ready a tray lined with several layers of kitchen paper. Mix together the ingredients for the cinnamon sugar in a wide bowl.

If you don't have a cooking thermometer, you can test if the oil is hot enough by dropping in a little bit of the dough (or a small piece of bread); it should sizzle immediately. Fry the churros in small batches: pipe short pieces of dough, about 1–2cm long, directly into the oil, using kitchen scissors to snip off the dough as you pipe. Fry each batch for 1½–2 minutes on each side or until golden brown all over. Remove the churros with a slotted spoon and tip on to the kitchen paper to drain. When all the churros have been fried, and while they are still hot, toss them in the cinnamon sugar to coat all over. Leave to cool.

Just before serving, add a layer of chocolate soil to each glass of chocolate mousse. Set the glasses on serving plates and serve with the vanilla churros on the side.

RESTAURANT DESSERTS

CHAMPAGNE-POACHED PEACHES WITH VANILLA YOGHURT TERRINE

This vanilla yoghurt terrine is a lighter form of the Italian pannacotta and it serves as the perfect canvas for fresh peaches that have been lightly poached in champagne. If you can't plump for champagne, poach the peaches in any white sparkling wine or Prosecco. You could also substitute the peaches with other stone fruit, such as nectarines, plums and apricots, or even fresh strawberries or pineapple. This is on the menu at Berner's Tavern as 'Peaches and cream'.

SERVES 8

For the vanilla yoghurt terrine
8 gelatine leaves
180g caster sugar
500ml double cream
1 vanilla pod, split in half, seeds
    scraped out with a knife
500ml Greek or natural yoghurt
45ml lime juice, strained

For the poached peaches
5 peaches
750ml bottle of Prosecco (or
    Champagne)
250ml maple syrup
1 vanilla pod, split in half, seeds
    scraped out with a knife

To assemble
2 ripe peaches
icing sugar, for dusting
Peach Sorbet (see page 203)

First, make the terrine. Lightly grease a 23cm square cake tin and line it with cling film. Soak the gelatine in a bowl of cold water for a few minutes. Meanwhile, put the sugar, cream and vanilla seeds in a pan and stir over medium heat just until the sugar has dissolved (take the pan off the heat before the cream begins to boil). Squeeze out any excess water from the gelatine leaves, then add to the warm cream and stir until melted. Add the yoghurt and lime juice and mix well. Pour the mixture into the prepared tray. Cover with cling film and chill for at least 4 hours or until the terrine has set.

Meanwhile, poach the peaches. Cut each peach in half and remove the stone. Put the Prosecco, maple syrup and vanilla pod and seeds into a wide pan (the peach halves should be able to fit in one layer). Stir over medium-high heat until the liquid begins to simmer. Add the peach halves and place a scrunched-up piece of greaseproof paper on top to keep them submerged. Poach for 8–10 minutes or until the peaches are tender – there should be little resistance when you pierce them with the tip of a small knife. Remove the pan from the heat and leave the peaches to cool in the poaching syrup.

Once cooled, remove the peaches with a slotted spoon and carefully peel off the skin. Return the peeled peaches to the syrup and keep in the fridge until ready to serve.

When ready to assemble the dessert, halve the two ripe peaches and remove the stones. Thinly slice one peach half and cut the rest into wedges. Lay the peach wedges on a baking sheet, dust with icing sugar and run a blowtorch over them until they are caramelised around the edges.

Transfer the terrine from the tray to a chopping board. Use a warm wet knife to cut out neat rectangles, each one about 12 x 3cm. Place a rectangle of terrine on each serving plate. Cut the poached peaches in half and arrange these on the plates with the caramelised fresh peaches. Garnish the plates with the thinly sliced peach. Finally, top the yoghurt terrine with a neat scoop of sorbet and serve immediately.

LEMON MERINGUE PIE WITH LEMONADE PARFAIT, BLACK PEPPER PASTRY AND SOUR YOGHURT

This is my take on the classic lemon meringue pie. It looks nothing like the original but offers the wonderful flavours of the traditional dessert with a few surprises thrown in.

SERVES 8

For the lemonade parfait
2 gelatine leaves
150ml lemon juice
20ml limoncello
155g caster sugar
150ml water
6 large egg yolks
2 large egg whites
175ml double cream
2–3 drops egg-yellow food colouring (optional)

For the lemon meringues
2 large egg whites (75g)
75g caster sugar
5g egg white powder
65ml lemon juice
60g icing sugar

For the black pepper pastry
160g unsalted butter, softened
80g caster sugar
¼ teaspoon coarsely ground black pepper
finely grated zest of 1 lemon
4 large egg yolks
25ml lemon juice
250g plain flour
1 tablespoon baking powder

For the yoghurt sherbet
50g icing sugar, sifted
25g yoghurt powder (available online from Amazon or other suppliers)

7g bicarbonate of soda
10g ascorbic acid

To serve
Lemon Curd (see page 243)

First make the lemonade parfait. Soak the gelatine leaves in a small bowl of cold water for a few minutes. Meanwhile, heat the lemon juice in a small saucepan to just below boiling point. Take the pan off the heat. Squeeze out the water from the gelatine leaves, then add to the pan and stir until the gelatine has melted. Stir in the limoncello. Set aside to cool completely.

Combine 75g of the sugar and 75ml of the water in a small heavy-based saucepan and warm over medium heat until the sugar has dissolved. Put a sugar thermometer into the pan, then increase the heat and boil the syrup to 118°C. Meanwhile, whisk the egg yolks in the bowl of an electric mixer fitted with the whisk attachment until the yolks are pale and thick. When the sugar syrup is ready, gradually trickle it into the egg yolks while whisking vigorously. When the syrup has been incorporated, continue to whisk until the mixture is light, fluffy and tripled in volume. The side of the bowl should no longer feel hot. This mixture is now referred to as a pâte à bombe. Set aside.

The meringue for the parfait is made using the same process, but you need to wash the beaters of the electric mixer first. Make a sugar syrup with the remaining 80g of sugar and 75ml water. Put a sugar thermometer in the pan and boil to 118°C. While the sugar syrup is boiling, whisk the egg whites in a clean, grease-free bowl to soft peaks, then gradually whisk in the

hot sugar syrup in a slow steady stream. Continue whisking until the meringue has tripled in volume and is thick and glossy.

In another bowl, whip the double cream to soft peaks. (If you want your parfait to be a pale yellow, add a few drops of yellow food colouring to the cream before whipping.) Now you are ready to assemble the parfait. Fold the lemon mixture into the pâte à bombe, then fold through the whipped cream. Finally, fold in the meringue until evenly combined. Divide the parfait mixture among eight individual moulds (we use cylindrical moulds but timbale or dariole moulds are fine too). Cover with cling film and freeze.

To make the lemon meringues, preheat the oven to 120°C/Fan 100°C/Gas Mark ½. Line two baking sheets with silicone mats or baking parchment. Put the egg whites into a clean bowl and whisk with an electric whisk to soft peaks. Mix together the caster sugar and egg white powder. Gradually whisk this into the egg whites, a tablespoon at a time and beating for a few seconds between each addition. Add the lemon juice and continue to whisk until the meringue is thick and glossy. Sift the icing sugar over the meringue and fold through.

Spread the meringue evenly on the lined baking sheets. Dry out in the oven for 1½–1¾ hours or until the meringues will come easily off the mat or baking parchment and sound crisp when tapped on the underside. Cool completely before breaking into shards. Keep between sheets of baking parchment in an airtight container.

To make the pastry, put the butter, sugar, black pepper and lemon zest into the bowl of an electric mixer fitted with the paddle attachment and beat on low speed until the mixture is pale and creamy. Gradually beat in the egg yolks, adding them one at a time, followed by the lemon juice. Sift in the flour and baking powder and fold them in thoroughly. Gather up the dough into a ball, then roll it out between two sheets of baking parchment to about 5mm thickness. Place on a baking sheet and chill for at least an hour.

Preheat the oven to 160°C/Fan 140°C/ Gas Mark 3. Peel off the top layer of parchment, then bake the pastry for 20–25 minutes or until golden brown. Cool completely before breaking into small pieces. Keep in an airtight container until ready to serve.

For the yoghurt sherbet, simply mix together all the dry ingredients and keep in an airtight container.

To assemble the dessert, spread some lemon curd in the middle of each serving plate. Scatter some black pepper pastry pieces over the curd. Unmould a lemonade parfait by dipping the mould into a bowl of hot water for 10 seconds (or running a blowtorch around the base and sides), then lay it on top of the pastry pieces. Sprinkle some yoghurt sherbet around the edge of the plate. Finish with a few shards of lemon meringue, then serve.

SOCIAL SWEETS

BASIL SORBET, STRAWBERRIES, YUZU YOGHURT AND BLACK PEPPER MERINGUE

The idea for this basil sorbet was something I picked up from Joel Robuchon many years ago. Basil may not seem like an obvious choice for a sorbet but it makes a fabulously refreshing sorbet with a gorgeous vivid green colour. Strawberries and basil have a natural affinity but I'm also including black pepper and a little creamy yoghurt to create the ultimate summer dessert.

SERVES 4

For the black pepper meringue
200g caster sugar
20g liquid glucose
80ml water
100g egg whites
1 tablespoon crushed black pepper

For the yuzu yoghurt mousse
2 gelatine leaves
25g caster sugar
25ml water
400g Greek yoghurt
130ml double cream
20ml yuzu juice (or fresh lime juice)
1 vanilla pod, split in half, seeds
  scraped out with a knife

To assemble
200g strawberries, hulled and
  quartered if large
Vanilla Stock Syrup (see page 242)
Green Basil Sorbet (see page 213)

First make the black pepper meringue. Preheat the oven to 120°C/Fan 100°C/Gas Mark ½. Line two baking sheets with silicone mats or baking parchment. Put the sugar, liquid glucose and water into a heavy-based saucepan and stir over medium heat until the sugar has dissolved. Put a sugar thermometer into the pan and increase the heat. Boil the syrup until it reaches 118°C.

While the syrup is boiling, beat the egg whites in the bowl of an electric mixer fitted with the whisk attachment. When the syrup is ready, gradually add it to the egg whites, whisking constantly, then continue to whisk the meringue until it has cooled slightly and the side of the bowl no longer feels very hot. The meringue should be thick, glossy and hold stiff peaks. Fold through the black pepper.

Spread the black pepper meringue thinly on the prepared baking sheets. Dry out in the oven for 1½–1¾ hours or until the meringue sheets will come easily off the mat or baking parchment and they sound crisp when tapped on the underside. Leave to cool completely before breaking into large pieces. Keep in an airtight container until ready to serve.

For the yuzu yoghurt mousse, soak the gelatine leaves in a small bowl of cold water for a few minutes. Meanwhile, stir the sugar and water together in a small saucepan over medium heat until the sugar has dissolved. Squeeze out the excess water from the gelatine leaves, then add to the pan and stir until melted. Strain the mixture through a sieve into a large measuring jug (or tall container). Leave to cool.

Add the yoghurt, cream, yuzu juice and vanilla seeds to the jug. Use a stick blender to blitz them together until smooth. Cover with cling film and chill for a few hours. Just before serving, blitz the mixture again with the stick blender until thick, then spoon into a piping bag fitted with a 1cm plain nozzle.

To assemble the dessert, pipe the yuzu yoghurt on to the centre of each serving plate. In a mixing bowl, toss the quartered strawberries with a little vanilla syrup, then arrange them around the yuzu yoghurt. Place a neat scoop of basil sorbet in the middle of the yoghurt. Quickly arrange the pieces of black pepper meringue around the strawberries and yoghurt, then drizzle a little vanilla syrup around each plate. Serve immediately.

CHOCOLATE AND STRAWBERRY ÉCLAIR WITH CHOCOLATE SORBET

Éclairs have quickly become our signature dessert at Berner's Tavern. They are always on our dessert menu though the fillings, toppings and accompanying ice cream or sorbet will change according to the seasons. In the winter, we would often flavour the éclairs with apples and pears flamed with Calvados. In the summer, we make this chocolate and strawberry version to take full advantage of beautiful British berries.

MAKES 28–30 ÉCLAIRS TO SERVE 14–15

1 quantity Choux Pastry (see page 239)

For the mascarpone cream
2½ gelatine leaves
450ml double cream
75g caster sugar
1 vanilla pod, split in half, seeds scraped out with a knife
225g mascarpone

For the strawberry jelly
250g very ripe (or thawed frozen) strawberries, hulled and roughly chopped
15g caster sugar
35ml Sugar Syrup (see page 242)
2½ gelatine leaves

For the chocolate crust
125g unsalted butter, softened
175g soft dark brown sugar
115g plain flour
140g ground almonds
30g cocoa powder

To assemble
750g fresh strawberries
edible gold or silver leaf (optional)
Chocolate Sorbet (see page 201) (optional)

First make the mascarpone cream. Soak the gelatine leaves in a bowl of cold water for a few minutes to soften. Meanwhile, heat the cream with the sugar and vanilla seeds and pod in a pan, stirring to dissolve the sugar. Before the cream starts to boil, take the pan off the heat. Squeeze out the excess water from the gelatine leaves, then add to the warm cream and stir until melted. Whisk in the mascarpone. Strain the mixture through a fine sieve into a large bowl. Cool completely, then refrigerate overnight to set.

For the strawberry jelly, put all the ingredients, except for the gelatine leaves, into a heatproof bowl and mix well, then set the bowl over a pan of gently simmering water. Poach, stirring occasionally, for 15–20 minutes or until the strawberries are soft and have released their juices. Remove the bowl from the pan.

Soak the gelatine leaves in a small bowl of cold water for a few minutes to soften. Pass the strawberries through a fine sieve into a bowl, pressing down on the pulp to extract as much juice as possible. Squeeze out the excess water from the gelatine leaves, then add to the warm strawberry juice and stir until melted. Pour into a small rectangular container. Cool completely, then cover and chill for at least 4 hours or until set. Before serving, cut the strawberry jelly into 1cm cubes.

For the chocolate crust, put the butter and sugar in the bowl of an electric mixer fitted with the paddle attachment (or you can use an electric whisk). Mix on low speed for a minute, then add the flour, ground almonds and cocoa powder. Continue mixing on low speed until the mixture comes together. Gather the dough and shape it to a rough rectangle. Place it on a baking sheet lined with a silicone mat or baking parchment and lay a large sheet of parchment on top. Roll out the dough very thinly (about 2mm thickness), then use a long chef's knife to mark out strips measuring 10 x 2cm. Freeze the strips for at least 30 minutes or until ready to use.

Preheat the oven to 190°C/Fan 170°C/Gas Mark 5. Line a large baking sheet with greaseproof paper. Prepare the choux pastry batter, then spoon it into a piping bag fitted with a 1.25–1.5cm wide plain nozzle. Pipe on to the baking sheet in 11cm lengths, leaving about 4cm of space between each one. Remove the chocolate crust from the freezer and use a small palette knife to carefully lift each one up and lay it on a piped choux length.

Bake the pastries for 10 minutes, then, without opening the oven door, turn the temperature down to 170°C/Fan 150°C/Gas Mark 3. Continue to bake for 15–20 minutes or until the pastries are dark golden brown and crisp. Remove from the oven and carefully make a hole at the base of each pastry. Place them back on the baking sheet and return to the oven to bake for 3–5 minutes (this will allow any trapped steam to escape and prevent the pastry from becoming soggy). Leave to cool on wire racks.

When you are ready to assemble the éclairs, whisk the mascarpone cream to loosen it, then spoon into a piping bag fitted with a 1cm fluted nozzle. Hull the strawberries and slice lengthways. Cut each pastry éclair lengthways in half. Pipe swirls of mascarpone cream on the bottom halves, then arrange the strawberry slices on this. Set the top halves of the éclairs in place.

Put a couple of filled chocolate and strawberry éclairs on each serving plate.

Garnish the top of each éclair with a row of strawberry jelly cubes and some gold leaf, if using. Serve immediately with a bowl of chocolate sorbet alongside, if you wish.

RESTAURANT DESSERTS

'WAGON WHEEL' TOASTED MARSHMALLOW, SALTED CARAMEL, RASPBERRY AND CHOCOLATE

The Wagon Wheel was one of my childhood tuck-shop favourites and this dessert is a fantastic grown-up version of the chocolate-coated cookie and marshmallow sandwich. Here, I'm also taking inspiration from the American 'S'mores' cookies by toasting the homemade marshmallow. The results are amazing and my two young daughters love this dessert as much as I do. It is quite a complicated dessert to get right, but if you do, it is a heap of fun!

SERVES 8–10

For the vanilla sablés
125g unsalted butter, softened
30g icing sugar, sifted
½ vanilla pod, split in half, seeds
   scraped out with a knife
125g plain flour

For the marshmallows
4 tablespoons cornflour
4 tablespoons icing sugar
225ml water
15g powdered gelatine
250g caster sugar
25g liquid glucose
2 medium egg whites

For the salted caramel sauce
125g caster sugar
15g unsalted butter
a pinch of fine sea salt
85ml double cream

For the tempered chocolate discs
100g dark chocolate (with 70% cocoa
   solids), chopped

To serve
Raspberry Jam (see page 245)
Raspberry and Yuzu Sorbet (see page
   207)
100–150g fresh raspberries, halved
Vanilla Stock Syrup (see page 424), for
   drizzling

First make the vanilla sablés. Put the softened butter and icing sugar into a mixing bowl and beat with a wooden spoon until evenly combined. Add the vanilla seeds and mix well. Sift in the flour and fold through until the mixture comes together into a soft dough. Scrape the dough on to a large piece of cling film and pat it out to a flat circle, then wrap well and chill for at least 30 minutes or until firm.

Unwrap the dough and roll it out between sheets of greaseproof paper to the thickness of a £1 coin. Use a large 10cm pastry cutter (or a small round saucer as a guide) to cut out discs. Arrange the pastry discs on a large baking sheet. Chill for 20 minutes to allow them to firm up before baking.

Preheat the oven to 180°C/Fan 160°C/ Gas Mark 4. Bake the sablé discs for 12–14 minutes or until they are lightly golden around the edge. Leave to cool completely on the baking sheet. If making ahead, store the sablés in an airtight container.

To make the marshmallows, start by preparing the baking sheet. Draw 8–10 circles, each measuring about 8cm in diameter, on a piece of baking parchment, then flip the parchment over on to a large baking sheet so that the pencil marks are on the underside of the parchment. Stir together the cornflour and icing sugar, then sift this mixture evenly over the parchment. Set aside.

Put 125ml of the water into a small saucepan and sprinkle over the gelatine. Leave to 'sponge' for a few minutes. Meanwhile, put the sugar, liquid glucose and remaining water into a small heavy-based saucepan and stir over medium-low heat until the sugar has dissolved. Place a sugar thermometer in the pan, then increase the heat and let the sugar syrup boil vigorously until it reaches 130°C. This will take 7–10 minutes.

Once the gelatine has swelled, set the pan over low heat and swirl the mixture until the gelatine has dissolved and the liquid is clear. Leave to cool slightly.

When the sugar syrup reaches 125°C, begin to whisk the egg whites in the bowl of an electric mixer fitted with the whisk attachment. Whisk the whites at high speed until they are thick and stiff. When the sugar syrup is at 130°C, take the pan off the heat. With the mixer still on high speed, slowly trickle the hot syrup on to the egg whites, taking care not to pour the syrup directly on to the beaters. Once all the syrup has been incorporated, slowly pour the gelatine on to the whites as you whisk. Continue to whisk for 10–15 minutes or until the marshmallow is thick and shiny and the side of the bowl no longer feels hot to the touch.

Whilst still warm, spoon the marshmallow into a piping bag fitted with a 1cm plain nozzle. Pipe neat rounds on the prepared baking sheet, within the marked circles. Put the baking sheet into the fridge to chill for at least 30 minutes or until the marshmallows have set.

For the salted caramel sauce, put the sugar into a heavy-based pan and set it over high heat. When the sugar begins to melt around the edges, tilt the pan from side to side to encourage the sugar to melt evenly. Let the sugar syrup caramelise to an amber colour, then quickly take the pan off the heat and add the butter and salt. Swirl to combine, then add the cream. (If any caramel hardens upon contact with the cream, simply return the pan to the heat and stir until the hardened caramel melts and the sauce is smooth.) Strain the sauce through a fine sieve into a jug. Cool before pouring into a squeezy bottle. Keep in the fridge until ready to serve.

For the chocolate discs, line a baking sheet with a silicone mat. Set aside a small handful of the chopped chocolate and put the rest into a heatproof bowl. Set the bowl over a pan of gently simmering water and melt the chocolate, stirring occasionally. Stick a chocolate (or sugar) thermometer into the chocolate and let it heat to 55°C. Take the bowl off the pan and add the reserved chocolate pieces. Stir until melted. Let the temperature of the melted chocolate cool to 27°C, then return the bowl to the pan of simmering water and bring the temperature of the chocolate up to 31°C.

Spread the tempered chocolate on the prepared baking sheet to 2–3mm thickness. Before the chocolate begins to set, use a 10cm pastry ring to mark out neat discs. Leave to cool and set on the silicone mat before peeling off the discs. Keep them in between sheets of baking parchment in an airtight container.

To assemble the dessert, squeeze a little salted caramel sauce on to the centre of each serving plate, then place a vanilla sablé disc on top. Spoon a little raspberry jam on to the vanilla sablé and top with a marshmallow round. Run a blowtorch over the top of the marshmallow until it is caramelised and toasted. Place a neat scoop or quenelle of sorbet in the middle and garnish with a few raspberry halves. Lean a tempered chocolate disc on the side and drizzle it with a little vanilla syrup. Serve at once.

PEACHES WITH RASPBERRY, GRANOLA AND PUFF PASTRY ICE CREAM

This fun, summery dessert was our way of combining the flavours of a raspberry tart and peach crumble together. Once you've mastered the art of making a simple vanilla ice cream, you can then have a lot of fun infusing the custard base with a whole variety of flavours to include atypical ingredients such as puff pastry. This extraordinary puff pastry ice cream adds a delicious element of surprise to the dessert and it ties all the elements of the pudding together. On this occasion, I would recommend using a shop-bought all butter puff pastry to make the ice cream. To save a bit of time, you can substitute good-quality store-bought vanilla ice cream for the puff pastry ice cream. Use any extra raspberry curd, granola or peach purée as a topping for ice cream or over breakfast muesli.

SERVES 6–8

For the flaked almond and pumpkin seed granola
40g demerara sugar
170g flaked almonds
40g pumpkin seeds
2 tablespoons lightly beaten egg whites

For the peach balls
3 just ripe peaches (preferably yellow, but white or flat peaches are fine too)
100g caster sugar
100ml peach liqueur

For the white peach purée
3 white peaches
100g caster sugar
4 teaspoons lemon juice

To assemble
Raspberry Curd (see page 243)
150g raspberries
12–16 baked puff pastry discs (from making Puff Pastry Ice Cream, page 183), dusted with icing sugar
Puff Pastry Ice Cream (see page 183)

To make the granola, preheat the oven to 180°C/Fan 160°C/Gas Mark 3. Combine all the ingredients in a mixing bowl and mix well. Spread out the mixture on a baking tray lined with a silicone mat or baking parchment and bake for 10–12 minutes or until golden brown, stirring the mixture halfway through baking. Remove from the oven and leave to cool completely. Keep in an airtight container until ready to serve.

For the peach balls, peel the peaches and remove the stones, then use a mini melon baller to scoop out as many neat balls from the flesh as possible. Set aside. Put the sugar into a small pan and set over medium heat. Without stirring, let the sugar melt and caramelise. You can tip the pan slightly from side to side to help it melt and caramelise evenly. When the caramel has turned golden brown, take the pan off the heat. Carefully add the peach liqueur, standing back as the hot caramel will spit and splutter upon contact with the cold liquid.

Add the peach balls, then boil for a few minutes to cook off some of the alcohol. Drain the peach balls in a sieve held over a bowl. Keep the peaches in a container in the fridge. Save the caramel to drizzle over the dessert. (If you think the caramel is too thin, boil it until reduced to a syrupy consistency, then cool.) Transfer the caramel to a small jar or squeezy bottle and keep in the fridge.

For the peach purée, peel the peaches, then cut the flesh into 1cm dice. Place in a pan and add the sugar and lemon juice. Cook over a medium heat until the peaches are soft. Tip the mixture into a blender and blitz to a purée. Pass the purée through a fine sieve. (If you think the purée is too thin, boil it for a few minutes until thickened to the desired consistency.) Keep in a jar or squeezy bottle in the fridge.

To assemble the dessert, randomly place little mounds of raspberry curd and peach purée around each serving plate. Scatter some granola on the peach purée, then add a few peach balls and raspberries to the plate. Place a small piece of puff pastry on one side of the plate and top it with a neat scoop of ice cream. Garnish the ice cream with another piece of puff pastry. Serve immediately.

ENGLISH STRAWBERRY BAKEWELL WITH AMARETTO AND HIBISCUS

This is a modern restaurant interpretation of the bakewell tart and I believe it to be just as good as the classic version, if not better. It has everything you would want from a dessert and it is best made in the summer when fresh British strawberries are in season.

SERVES 10

For the almond sponge
50g unsalted butter, plus extra for greasing
3 medium eggs
80g caster sugar
½ vanilla pod, split in half, seeds scraped out with a knife
20g plain flour
a pinch of fine sea salt
50g ground almonds

For the almond bricelet
65g unsalted butter
25ml double cream
75g caster sugar
2g powdered pectin
25g liquid glucose
50g flaked almonds

For the marzipan
250g toasted flaked almonds
½ teaspoon fine sea salt
125g icing sugar
finely grated zest of 1 lemon
25ml water

For the strawberry compote
500g strawberries (thawed if frozen), hulled and roughly chopped
150g caster sugar
½ vanilla pod, split in half, seeds scraped out with a knife
10g powdered pectin

To assemble
150g fresh strawberries, hulled and thinly sliced
a handful of baby basil leaves
Strawberry and Hibiscus Sorbet (see page 199)

First, prepare the almond sponge. Preheat the oven to 180°C/Fan 160°C/Gas Mark 4. Grease a 20cm square baking tin and line with baking parchment.

Melt the butter in a small saucepan over medium heat, then let the butter continue to heat until it turns golden brown and smells nutty. Strain the butter through a fine sieve into a bowl and leave to cool. Meanwhile, put the eggs, sugar and vanilla seeds in the bowl of an electric mixer fitted with the whisk attachment. Whisk the mixture for 5–10 minutes or until it is light and fluffy and has tripled in volume. Sift together the flour, salt and ground almonds, then add to the egg mixture and gently fold in followed by the cooled browned butter.

Pour the sponge mixture into the prepared tin and spread evenly; level the top with a spatula. Bake for about 20 minutes or until a skewer inserted into the middle of the sponge comes out clean. Remove from the oven (leave the oven on) and cool completely. Once cold, unmould the sponge and cut into 10 x 4cm pieces. Store

the sponge pieces (layered between sheets of baking parchment) in a cake tin or other airtight container until ready to serve.

Next, make the almond bricelet. Line a baking sheet with a large silicone mat. Put the ingredients except for the almonds in a heavy-based saucepan and stir over medium heat until the sugar has dissolved and the mixture is smooth. Increase the heat slightly and boil for a few minutes; stir frequently as the sugary mixture can catch and burn easily. Remove from the heat, tip in the almonds and stir until the almonds are evenly coated.

Spread the mixture on the lined baking sheet. To get the bricelet really thin, place a sheet of baking parchment on top and roll the mixture out to the thickness of the almonds. Remove the parchment and bake for about 10–13 minutes or until evenly golden brown.

Remove the bricelet from the oven and leave to cool for a couple of minutes. While still warm, cut out 10 neat strips the same size as the almond sponge (10 x 4cm). Leave to cool on the baking sheet: the bricelet will become crisp and brittle. Keep in an airtight container until ready to serve.

For the marzipan, combine all the ingredients in a bowl. Mix well and press to a firm paste. Roll out the marzipan between sheets of greaseproof paper to 3mm thickness, then freeze for about 30 minutes or until firm. Cut the marzipan into 10 strips (10 x 4cm). Keep between sheets of greaseproof paper in an airtight container until ready to serve.

To make the strawberry compote, put all the ingredients in a pan and heat gently until the sugar dissolves. Bring to a simmer, then cover the pan and cook for a couple of minutes until the strawberries are dark red and syrupy. Cool completely, then keep in a sealed container in the fridge (for up to a week if preparing ahead).

To assemble each bakewell 'tart', place a strip of marzipan in the centre of a serving plate. Spread a teaspoonful of strawberry compote on the marzipan, then place a piece of almond sponge on top. Spread a little more strawberry compote on the sponge and cover with a layer of overlapped strawberry slices. Top with a

piece of almond bricelet. Dot little mounds of strawberry compote around the plate. Garnish these and the bakewell with fresh baby basil leaves. Finally, add a neat scoop or quenelle of sorbet to the plate and serve immediately.

RESTAURANT DESSERTS

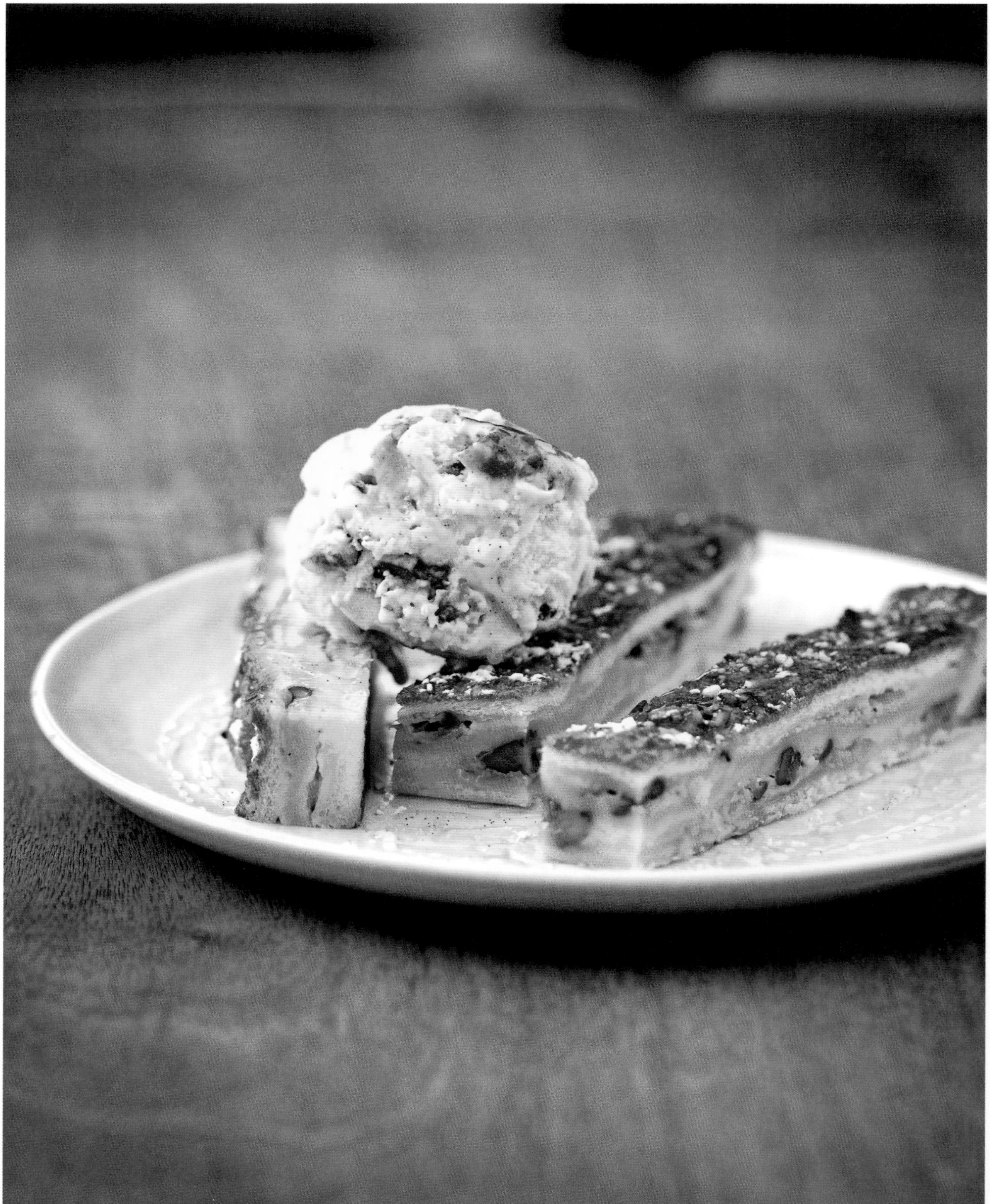

BREAD AND BUTTER PUDDING WITH VANILLA AND PECAN ICE CREAM

This version of bread and butter pudding is quite rich but it is splendid with the vanilla and pecan ice cream. It also works well with sea salt and almond or salted caramel ice creams (see pages 185 and 186).

SERVES 8–10

For the bread and butter pudding
150g unsalted butter, softened, plus
    extra for greasing
375ml double cream
25g smooth peanut butter
225g white chocolate chips
35g soft light brown sugar
2 firm but ripe bananas
1 large egg
1 large egg yolk
1 small (or ½ large) stale loaf of
    sliced white bread, crusts removed
75g toasted pecans, roughly chopped
3–4 tablespoons warmed apricot jam,
    for glazing

To serve
Vanilla and Pecan Ice Cream (see
    page 181)

To make the bread and butter pudding, preheat the oven to 170°C/Fan 150°C/ Gas Mark 3. Lightly butter a deep 1.5–2 litre ovenproof dish, then line the base with baking parchment.

Put the cream and peanut butter into a heavy-based saucepan and give the mixture a stir. Set the pan over high heat and bring to the boil. Meanwhile, put half the white chocolate chips into a large bowl. When the cream starts to boil, pour it over the chocolate and stir until the chocolate has melted and the mixture is smooth. Leave to cool.

Melt 50g of the butter in another heavy-based pan over medium-high heat. When the butter begins to foam, add the sugar and stir until it dissolves. Peel and slice the bananas, then add them to the pan. Fry until golden brown and caramelised, then flip the slices over and fry on the other side for 1–2 minutes. Remove to a plate and leave to cool.

Lightly beat together the egg, egg yolk and peanut butter cream, then strain the mixture through a sieve into a jug. Cut the bread slices in half diagonally to make triangles. Butter them, then arrange in the prepared dish, adding the caramelised bananas, remaining white chocolate chips and half the pecans in between the layers. Pour half the cream and egg mixture evenly over the top and let the bread soak up the liquid for a few minutes before pouring over the remaining mixture. Sprinkle the rest of the pecans on top.

Bake for 25–35 minutes or until the pudding has set and is lightly golden brown. Leave to cool completely, then run a knife around the inside edge and invert the pudding on to a large piece of cling film. Wrap well and freeze for half an hour or until the pudding is firm.

Unwrap the pudding and cut into thin slices. Melt a good knob of butter in a wide frying pan and fry the pudding slices for 1–1½ minutes on each side or until golden brown. Remove to a plate, then brush with the apricot jam to glaze.

To serve, place a few of slices of bread pudding on each serving plate and top with a scoop of ice cream.

GREEN TEA CAKE, YUZU AND RASPBERRIES

My chefs in Asia are crazy about matcha powder and they are always inventing new ways to incorporate green tea into their dishes. This one was created by my pastry chef at Commune Social in Shanghai and it is a rather simple but elegant dessert combining the Japanese flavours of green tea and yuzu with creamy yoghurt and raspberries.

SERVES 10

For the green tea cake
60ml vegetable oil, plus extra for
    greasing
125g plain flour
1½ teaspoons baking powder
½ teaspoon fine sea salt
1 tablespoon matcha (green tea)
    powder
110g caster sugar
2 medium eggs
a few drops of vanilla extract
125ml natural yoghurt

For the green tea honeycomb
250g caster sugar
100ml water
25g bicarbonate of soda
½ teaspoon matcha (green tea)
    powder

To serve
250–300g fresh raspberries
1 yuzu (or lemon), for zesting
Raspberry and Yuzu Sorbet (see page
    207)

First make the green tea cake. Preheat the oven to 160°C/Fan 140°C/Gas Mark 3. Grease a 23cm square cake tin and line with baking parchment. Sift the flour, baking powder, salt and matcha powder into a bowl. In another bowl, combine the sugar, eggs, vanilla extract and oil and beat with an electric whisk until the mixture is pale and light. In alternate small batches, gently fold in the dry ingredients and the natural yoghurt until evenly incorporated, taking care not to overwork the mixture.

Spread the mixture in the prepared cake tin. Bake for 20–25 minutes or until the cake is light golden brown on top and a skewer inserted into the middle comes out clean. Leave to cool for a few minutes, then unmould the cake on to a wire rack and let it cool completely. For serving, peel off the baking parchment and slice the cake into 10 portions.

To make the green tea honeycomb, put the sugar and water into a heavy-based saucepan and stir over medium heat until the sugar has dissolved. Increase the heat to high and let the sugar syrup boil until it reaches 130°C on a sugar thermometer. It should have turned to an amber-coloured caramel. While the syrup is boiling, stir together the bicarbonate of soda and matcha powder. Line a baking sheet with a silicone mat.

When the sugar syrup has reached the right temperature, take the pan off the heat and tip in the matcha mixture. Immediately stir the mixture with a heatproof spatula – the sugar syrup will foam and increase in volume. Quickly pour it on to the lined baking sheet. If necessary, tilt the baking sheet from side to side to even out the thickness of the honeycomb. Leave to cool for an hour or so: the honeycomb will harden and become brittle. Once it has set, break it into small pieces and store in an airtight container until ready to serve.

To assemble the dessert, put a slice of green tea cake on each serving plate and arrange some raspberries on top. Crush some green tea honeycomb into fine crumbs and sprinkle a little over the raspberries. Place a neat pile of green tea honeycomb crumbs next to the cake, then top it with a neat scoop or quenelle of sorbet. Finely grate a little yuzu zest over the raspberries and cake. Serve immediately.

RESTAURANT DESSERTS

RED DOT BREWHOUSE SAUVIGNON ALE, YEAST, HOPS, COCOA PRETZEL AND APRICOTS

There is an independent microbrewery in Singapore called Red Dot that produces a beautifully balanced light ale infused with sauvignon grapes so it has notes of both beer and wine. My pastry chef wanted to recreate this unique flavour profile in a dessert and this was the impressive result. The sauvignon ale is infused into a white chocolate-coated mousse shaped into a sphere, and this is served with hops-flavoured sponge, beer yeast ice cream, chocolate and pretzel crumbs and apricot purée. Admittedly, it is a rather complicated dessert to make and you would have to order specialist ingredients such as hops and beer yeast from a homebrew supplier but if you manage to pull it off, it will be the talk of the town! Sauvignon ale is hard to find outside of Singapore so substitute it with any pale, golden ale.

SERVES 8–10

For the ale mousse
100g caster sugar
2 medium egg whites
180ml Sauvignon Ale (or any pale ale)
6g powdered gelatine
145ml double cream
300g white chocolate, chopped

For the hops sponge
75ml vegetable oil, plus extra for greasing
2.5g dried hops
125ml whole milk
3 medium eggs
180g caster sugar

110g liquid glucose, warmed
185g plain flour
1 teaspoon baking powder

For the chocolate pretzel crumb
60g unsalted butter, softened
60g caster sugar
1 medium egg white
65g plain flour
a pinch of fine sea salt
25g cocoa powder
245g honey mustard and onion pretzels (we use Snyder's)

For the cocoa gelée
300ml cocoa liqueur (such as crème de cacao)
2g agar agar powder
25g caster sugar

For the apricot gel
350g fresh apricots, halved and stoned
95g caster sugar
75ml water
2g agar agar powder

To serve
Yeast Ice Cream (see page 184)

First make the ale mousse. Put the sugar into a heavy-based saucepan with a small splash of water and stir over medium heat until the sugar dissolves. Increase the heat and boil the sugar syrup until it reaches 120°C. Meanwhile, put the egg whites into the bowl of an electric mixer fitted with the whisk attachment and whisk to stiff peaks. When the sugar syrup has reached the right temperature, slowly trickle it on to the whites while whisking constantly. Continue to whisk until the meringue is thick and

glossy and the side of the bowl no longer feels hot.

While the meringue is being whisked, pour a third of the ale into a small saucepan and sprinkle over the gelatine. Leave the gelatine to 'sponge' for a few minutes, then heat the mixture over medium heat until the gelatine dissolves. Leave to cool slightly before stirring in the rest of the ale.

Add the ale mixture to the meringue and fold through. Whip the double cream to medium peaks, then fold into the ale and meringue mixture. Spoon into 16–20 flexible half-sphere moulds. Freeze them for a few hours or until firm. (If you don't have sphere moulds, you can freeze the mixture in a shallow container until set, then use an ice cream scoop to scoop out neat round balls; refreeze the balls until firm.)

When you are ready to assemble the spheres, line a baking sheet with a silicone mat. Melt the white chocolate in a heatproof bowl set over a pan of gently simmering water. Remove from the pan and leave to cool slightly. Unmould two frozen mousse halves and press them together to form a sphere. Stick a skewer through the halves to hold them together, then dip in the melted chocolate to coat. Tap the skewer to shake off any excess chocolate, then set the coated sphere on the lined baking sheet. Continue forming and coating the rest of the spheres. If the chocolate sets too quickly, put it over the pan of water to melt before using again. When all the spheres have been coated in chocolate, keep them in the fridge until ready to serve.

(continued on page 136)

For the hops sponge, preheat the oven to 180°C/Fan 160°C/Gas Mark 4. Grease a 23cm square baking tin and line with baking parchment. Put the hops and milk into a small saucepan and bring to the boil. Remove from the heat and leave to infuse for 10 minutes, then strain the milk through a fine sieve and discard the hops.

Put the eggs and sugar in the bowl of an electric mixer fitted with the whisk attachment and whisk until light and fluffy. Add the liquid glucose and vegetable oil and fold through. Sift together the flour and baking powder, then fold alternately into the egg mixture with the hop-infused milk.

Pour the sponge mixture into the prepared cake tin. Bake for 40–45 minutes or until the sponge is golden brown and a skewer inserted into the centre comes out clean. Cool slightly, then unmould the sponge on to a wire rack and leave to cool completely. (Leave the oven on for the chocolate pastry.) Once cold, freeze the sponge for about an hour or until firm, then cut into thin 3cm-long strips. Store in a cake tin until ready to serve.

For the chocolate pretzel crumb, line a baking sheet with a silicone mat. Cream the butter and sugar together until the mixture is light and fluffy. Add the egg white and beat to combine. Sift the flour, salt and cocoa powder into the bowl, then fold into the creamed mixture to form a dough. Scrape the dough on to the lined baking sheet. Lay a sheet of baking parchment on top and roll out the dough to the thickness of a £1 coin. Remove the parchment and bake for 12–13 minutes or until the

chocolate pastry is golden brown. Leave to cool completely.

Break the chocolate pastry into small pieces and transfer to a food processor. Add the pretzels and blitz to fine crumbs. Store in an airtight container until ready to serve.

For the cocoa gelée, put all the ingredients into a small saucepan and stir over medium heat until the sugar and agar agar have dissolved. Bring to the boil, then take the pan off the heat and leave to cool. Pour the mixture into a shallow container, cover and chill for a couple of hours or until set. For serving, cut into small cubes.

For the apricot gel, put the apricot halves in a saucepan with the sugar and water. Shake the pan to combine, then set over medium-high heat and bring to a simmer. Leave to poach, uncovered, for 10–15 minutes or until the apricots are soft. Tip the hot apricots and juices into a food processor and blitz until smooth. Pass the apricot purée through a fine sieve back into the pan. Add the agar agar powder and stir in. Bring to the boil, then take the pan off the heat and leave to cool. Transfer the apricot mixture to a wide square or rectangular container, cover and chill until set. Once set, put the apricot gel into a food processor and blitz until smooth. Spoon the gel into a piping bag fitted with a small plain nozzle and set aside until ready to serve.

To assemble the dessert, spoon a little chocolate pretzel crumb on to the centre of each serving plate. Place two strips of hops sponge alongside, then pipe two little mounds of apricot gel on to the plate.

Arrange eight to ten cubes of cocoa gelée randomly on the plate. Finally, place an ale mousse sphere and a neat scoop of yeast ice cream on top of the chocolate pretzel crumbs and serve immediately.

MATCHA, STRAWBERRY, SOUR PLUM AND TAHINI CREAM ('MATCHA')

This lovely and light dessert is dairy-free and it showcases typical Japanese ingredients such as matcha (green tea), umeboshi (sour plum), goma (tahini) and sake. Since the sponge is fat-free, it will dry out quickly and is best consumed within a day or two. If you are short of time, leave out the matcha marshmallows and strawberry paper.

SERVES 8–10

For the steamed matcha sponge
flavourless oil for greasing
4 large eggs
180g caster sugar
230g plain flour
2 teaspoons matcha (green tea) powder
75ml strong sake

For the matcha syrup
35g loose matcha tea leaves
250ml boiling water
100g caster sugar
50ml sake

For the sour plum gel
250g plums
50ml balsamic vinegar
1 teaspoon sea salt
3g agar agar powder

For the tahini cream
25g thick-set honey
125g tahini
150ml double cream
3g agar agar powder

For the matcha marshmallows
3g matcha (green tea) powder
6g powdered gelatine
135g caster sugar
25g liquid glucose
50ml water
1½ medium egg whites
3 tablespoons cornflour mixed with 3 tablespoons icing sugar, for dusting

For the strawberry paper
250g strawberries, hulled and roughly chopped
20g caster sugar
4g powdered pectin

To serve (optional)
sansho pepper, for sprinkling
umeboshi powder (optional) (available online from www. macrobioticshop.co.uk)
matcha (green tea) powder, for sprinkling
20 large strawberries, hulled and quartered lengthways
Strawberry and Sake Sorbet (see page 202)

To make the matcha sponge, preheat the oven to 140°C/Fan 120°C/Gas Mark 1. If it isn't a steam oven, place a baking tray half-filled with water on the bottom shelf of the oven when you turn it on. Grease a 20cm square baking tin and line with baking parchment.

In a large bowl, whisk the eggs with the sugar using an electric whisk until the mixture is pale, light and tripled in volume. Sift in the flour and matcha powder. Gently fold through, then add the sake and fold again. Pour the sponge mixture into the prepared tin and bake in the steamy oven for 30–40 minutes or until the sponge has set and is slightly springy to the touch; a skewer inserted into the centre should come out clean.

Remove the sponge from oven and leave to cool slightly before turning out on to a wire rack. When completely cooled, store in a cake tin until ready to serve.

For the matcha syrup, put the matcha leaves, water and sugar in a small saucepan and stir over low heat until the sugar has dissolved. Remove from the heat and leave to steep and cool to room temperature, then strain through a fine sieve into a jug. Add the sake and stir well. Pour the matcha syrup into a small squeezy bottle and set aside.

For the sour plum gel, halve the plums and remove the stones, then roughly chop the flesh. Put into a pan with a tiny splash of water and simmer the plums for 5–10 minutes or until they are very soft. Tip the hot plums into a food processor and blitz until smooth. Return the purée to the pan and stir in the vinegar, salt and agar agar. Bring to the boil, then pour the mixture into a bowl or shallow tray. Leave to cool, then cover with cling film and chill for a few hours or until set. Once set, transfer the gel to a blender or food processor and blitz to make a consistency that will pipe easily. Spoon into a piping bag fitted with a 5mm plain nozzle or a squeezy bottle and keep in the fridge until ready to serve.

(continued on page 138)

For the tahini cream, put all the ingredients into a heavy-based saucepan and stir well, then bring just to the boil. Immediately pour the mixture into a wide bowl and leave to cool completely before covering with cling film. Chill for several hours or until set. As with the sour plum gel, blitz the set tahini cream in a food processor to a loose consistency, then spoon into a piping bag fitted with a 5mm plain nozzle or a squeezy bottle. Keep in the fridge until needed.

To make the matcha marshmallows, put the matcha powder into a small pan and stir in 3 tablespoons of hot water. Sprinkle the gelatine over the mixture and leave to 'sponge' for a few minutes, then stir over medium heat until the gelatine has dissolved and the liquid is clear. Set aside.

Put the sugar, liquid glucose and 50ml water into a heavy-based saucepan and stir over medium heat until the sugar has dissolved. Place a sugar thermometer in the pan, then increase the heat and boil the mixture to 120°C. Meanwhile, put the egg whites in the bowl of an electric mixer fitted with the whisk attachment and whisk at medium speed to stiff peaks. When the sugar syrup reaches the right temperature, increase the mixer speed to high and very slowly trickle the hot syrup on to the egg whites, whisking constantly. When fully incorporated, add the matcha and gelatine mixture and continue to whisk until the side of the bowl no longer feels hot.

Line a 23cm square cake tin with baking parchment, then sift half the cornflour and icing sugar mixture over the base to cover evenly. Spread the marshmallow mixture in the tin and even it out with a spatula. Dust the top with the rest of the cornflour and icing sugar mixture. Chill for 12 hours or overnight until set. For serving, remove from the tin and cut into small squares.

To make the strawberry paper, preheat the oven to 100°C/Fan 80°C/Gas Mark ¼, and line two baking sheets with silicone mats. Put the strawberries into a pan with a tiny splash of water and set on a high heat. Mix the sugar with the pectin, then add to the pan and give the mixture a stir. Bring to the boil and boil for about 5 minutes or until the strawberries are soft. Carefully tip the hot mixture into a blender and blitz until smooth (halfway through, stop the blender and scrape down the sides). Pass the purée through a fine sieve.

Divide the purée between the prepared baking sheets and use a palette knife to spread out to make a very thin, even rectangle on each sheet. Bake for 1 hour or until the strawberry paper feels dry to the touch. Turn off the oven and leave the paper inside to cool. Once cold, tear or cut the strawberry paper into long shards. Store in between sheets of baking parchment in an airtight container until ready to serve (the paper can be kept like this for a couple of days).

To assemble the dessert, cut the sponge into small pieces. (At the restaurant, we trim off the top 'skin' from the sponge but you can leave it on if you prefer.) Drizzle the matcha syrup over the pieces of sponge, then place a few pieces on each large serving plate. Lightly sprinkle each piece of sponge with a pinch of sansho pepper and a pinch of umeboshi powder. Smear little dots of plum gel and tahini cream around the plate. Dust a little matcha powder over the strawberry quarters, then arrange a few pieces on the plate along with some matcha marshmallows. Place a neat scoop or quenelle of sorbet in the middle of the plate and garnish with a few shards of strawberry paper. Serve immediately.

RESTAURANT DESSERTS

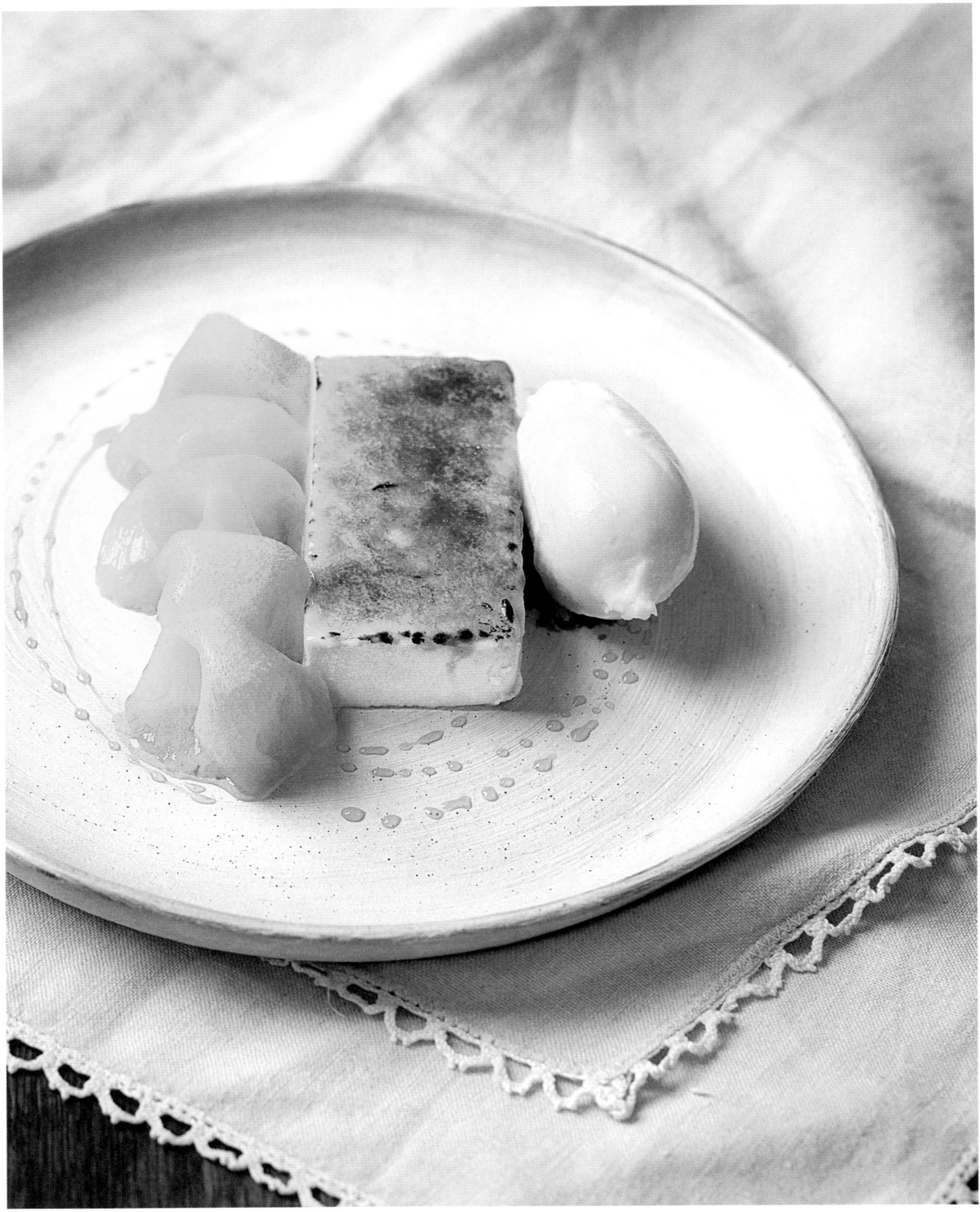

TOASTED COCONUT CRÈME BRÛLÉE WITH PINEAPPLE, COCONUT AND MALIBU SORBET

In this recipe, the classic crème brûlée is given a Caribbean twist based on the flavours of a piña colada. It is a wonderful dessert as the rich and creamy crème brûlée is balanced by the refreshing pineapple and coconut and Malibu sorbet. I'd happily eat the sorbet on its own so I'd always make a large batch to have extra in the freezer. Start preparing the dessert the day before you intend to serve it.

SERVES 6

For the coconut crème brûlée
65g desiccated coconut
450ml whole milk
250ml double cream
8 large egg yolks
50g caster sugar
6 teaspoons demerara sugar

For the pineapple in ginger and saffron syrup
50g fresh ginger, peeled and roughly chopped
100g caster sugar
a pinch of saffron threads
250ml white wine
1 small ripe pineapple, peeled, cored and thinly sliced

To serve
Coconut and Malibu Sorbet (see page 198)

Preheat the oven to 180°C/Fan 160°C/Gas Mark 4. Spread the desiccated coconut evenly on a baking sheet and toast in the oven for about 10 minutes, tossing once or twice, until the coconut is dark brown. Meanwhile, heat the milk in a saucepan. As soon as the coconut is ready, tip it into a heatproof bowl and pour in the hot milk. Leave to cool and infuse for about an hour.

Strain the coconut-infused milk through a fine sieve, pressing down on the coconut to extract as much milk as possible (you need 250ml milk for the crème brûlée). Chill overnight.

The next day, preheat the oven to 140°C/Fan 120°C/Gas Mark 1. Place six individual rectangular moulds (or 150ml ramekins) in a large, deep roasting tray. Bring a kettle of water to the boil.

If there is a layer of skin on top of the coconut-infused milk, skim this off. Pour the milk into a pan, add the cream and bring to the boil. Meanwhile, whisk together the egg yolks and sugar in a large heatproof bowl. Trickle the hot creamy milk over the mixture, whisking as you do so. When fully incorporated, strain the mixture through a fine sieve into a large jug.

Pour the creamy mixture into the moulds (or ramekins) until they are three-quarters full. Pull out the middle shelf of the oven slightly and carefully place the roasting tray on it, then pour enough boiling water into the tray to come halfway up the sides of the moulds. Gently push the shelf back into the oven and bake for 30–40 minutes or until the custards are just set but still a bit wobbly in the middle when you gently shake the tray.

Remove the moulds from the water and set aside to cool to room temperature, then keep in the fridge until ready to serve.

Next make the ginger and saffron syrup for the pineapple. Put the ginger in a small pan and cover with cold water. Bring to the boil, then immediately drain the ginger in a sieve. Return the blanched ginger to the pan and add the sugar, saffron and 150ml of the wine. Set over medium-to-high heat and stir to dissolve the sugar, then bring to the boil. Take the pan off the heat and stir in the remaining wine. Leave to cool completely, then strain the syrup through a sieve into a bowl (discard the ginger). Add the thinly sliced pineapple to the ginger and saffron syrup and leave to macerate for about an hour.

Just before serving, unmould each crème brûlée on to a serving plate. To do this, run a thin knife around the inside of the mould or ramekin, then invert on to the plate. Holding the plate and ramekin tightly together, give them a shake to release the crème brûlée on to the plate. (Alternatively, you can simply serve the crème brûlée in the ramekins.) Sprinkle the top of each crème brûlée with a thin, even layer of demerara sugar, then run a blowtorch over the sugar until it caramelises to a golden brown crust.

Drain the pineapple slices, reserving the ginger syrup. Arrange a few rolled-up slices of pineapple alongside each crème brûlée. Drizzle the ginger and saffron syrup around the plate. Finally, add a scoop of sorbet alongside the crème brûlée and serve immediately.

CRISPY LEMON MERINGUE, CUCUMBER SORBET AND GIN GEL

This refreshing dessert is based on the flavours of a classic gin and tonic but with an interesting combination of textures from the lemon meringue, dehydrated black olives, fresh mango, lemon and gin gel and cucumber sorbet. It is a particularly good dessert to follow a rich and heavy main course.

SERVES 8–10 (WITH EXTRA LEMON MERINGUES)

For the crispy lemon meringues
100g egg whites (from about 3
    medium eggs)
100g caster sugar
100g icing sugar
finely grated zest of 1 lemon

For the lemon and gin gel
125ml lemon juice
125ml water
50g caster sugar
1 teaspoon agar agar powder
40ml gin (such as Hendricks)

To serve
1 ripe mango, peeled and diced
dehydrated black olives, finely
    chopped (see **Crème Catalan**, page
    120)
Cucumber Sorbet (see page 195)

To make the crispy lemon meringues, preheat the oven to 120°C/Fan 100°C/Gas Mark ½. Line two baking sheets with silicone mats or baking parchment. Whisk the egg whites to soft peaks. With the electric whisk on high speed, slowly add the caster sugar a tablespoon at a time. Once all the caster sugar has been added, whisk the meringue back to stiff peaks. Sift the icing sugar, then add this and the lemon zest to the meringue. Fold in until well combined.

Spoon the lemon meringue into a large piping bag fitted with a 1cm plain nozzle. Pipe little round swirls of meringue on the prepared baking sheets, leaving about 2cm of space between each one to allow for expansion during baking. Dry out in the oven for 1–1½ hours or until the meringues are crisp and you can lift them cleanly off the silicone mat or parchment. Leave the meringues to cool completely, then store between sheets of baking parchment in an airtight container.

Next, make the lemon and gin gel. Pour the lemon juice and water into a heavy-based pan. Mix the sugar and agar agar together, then sprinkle this on top of the liquid in the pan. Set over medium-low heat and stir until the sugar and agar agar have dissolved. Increase the heat and bring to the boil. Take the pan off the heat and stir in the gin. Set aside to cool slightly before pouring the gel mixture into a shallow container or a small baking tray. Cover and chill for a few hours until set. Cut into small cubes to serve.

To assemble the dessert, lay out the crispy lemon meringues on a baking sheet (you need five or six per person) and run a blowtorch over them until the tips are browned. Place several lemon and gin gel cubes in the centre of each shallow serving bowl. Add a few cubes of mango around the gel, then arrange crispy lemon meringues around these. Scatter over some dehydrated black olives. Finally, place a neat scoop or quenelle of sorbet in the centre, on top of the gel cubes, and serve immediately.

RESTAURANT DESSERTS

COFFEE AND MANDARIN ('MANDARIN')

This is a sophisticated dessert featuring the unusual pairing of coffee and mandarin orange, which works beautifully. On its own, the coffee cake is lovely and moist but when savoured with coffee cream, roasted mandarin ice cream, mandarin gel and coffee meringues, it is a taste sensation. With the exception of the mandarin segments, you can prepare every component of this dessert a day in advance.

SERVES 5–6

For the coffee cream
1 teaspoon good-quality instant coffee granules
375ml double cream
½ teaspoon agar agar powder
175g caster sugar

For the coffee cake
35ml vegetable oil, plus extra for greasing
1 medium egg
1 medium egg yolk
90g caster sugar
55g liquid glucose, lightly warmed
45ml whole milk
2 teaspoons coffee extract
95g plain flour
½ teaspoon baking powder

For the mandarin gel
300g mandarin purée (we use Boiron purées)
½ teaspoon agar agar powder

For the coffee meringues
1 large egg white
24g egg white powder
65g icing sugar, sifted
2 teaspoons espresso powder

To serve
Candied Mandarin Peel (see page 241)
Maldon sea salt, for sprinkling
15–18 mandarin segments (without membrane)
Roasted Mandarin Ice Cream (see page 188)

For the coffee cream, put the coffee granules and half the cream into a heavy-based saucepan. Sprinkle over the agar agar. Set the pan on a medium heat and give the mixture a stir. Let it come to the boil, then remove from the heat.

Put the sugar into another heavy-based pan and place over high heat. When the sugar begins to melt, tilt the pan from side to side so that the sugar melts and caramelises evenly. As soon as the caramel turns a light amber colour, take the pan off the heat and carefully pour in the warm coffee cream. If some of the caramel hardens upon contact with the liquid, return the pan to the heat and stir until smooth. Strain the mixture through a sieve into a bowl, then stir in the rest of the cream. Cover with cling film and chill overnight.

The next day, lightly whip the coffee cream to soft peaks, then return to the fridge and chill for a couple of hours or until firm.

To make the coffee cake, preheat the oven to 160°C/Fan 140°C/Gas Mark 3. Grease a 23cm square cake tin and line with baking parchment. Put the egg, egg yolk, sugar and liquid glucose into the bowl of an electric mixer fitted with the whisk attachment and whisk until light and fluffy. With the mixer on high speed, slowly trickle in the milk and coffee extract. Sift together the flour and baking powder into the bowl and gently fold through. Add the oil and fold again until the mixture is just combined.

Pour the mixture into the prepared cake tin and level the top with a spatula. Bake for 45–55 minutes or until the cake is lightly golden brown and a skewer inserted into the centre comes out clean. Cool for a few minutes, then turn out on to a wire rack and leave to cool completely.

Shortly before serving, turn the cake over and place on a cutting board. Peel off the baking parchment, then cut the cake into neat squares or use a 4–5cm ring cutter to stamp out neat cylinders – you need three for each serving. (The latter method will leave you with cake trimmings, which you can enjoy as a cook's treat.) Or you can cut the cake into shapes as soon as it has cooled, and store these in an airtight container between sheets of baking parchment.

For the mandarin gel, put the purée and agar agar into a pan and stir over medium heat until the mixture boils. Pour it into a bowl and leave to cool completely, then cover with cling film and chill for at least 4 hours or until set.

(continued on page 146)

Transfer the gel to a small food processor and blitz on high speed for 1–2 minutes until it is light and smooth and has a consistency that can be piped. Spoon into a large piping bag fitted with a plain round nozzle about 5mm diameter. Keep in the fridge until ready to serve.

To make the coffee meringues, preheat the oven to 120°C/Fan 100°C/Gas Mark ½. Line two baking sheets with silicone mats or baking parchment. Put the egg white, egg white powder and sugar into a large heatproof bowl and whisk for a couple of minutes using an electric whisk until the mixture is light and fluffy. Set the bowl over a pan of simmering water and continue to whisk on high speed until the meringue is thick and shiny. Remove the bowl from the pan and carry on whisking until the side of the bowl no longer feels hot. Add the espresso powder and whisk until evenly incorporated.

Spread the meringue evenly on the prepared baking sheets. Dry out in the oven for 30–45 minutes or until the meringue can easily be lifted off the silicone mat or baking parchment. Leave to cool completely before breaking into smaller pieces. Keep in an airtight container until ready to use.

To assemble the dessert, place three pieces of coffee cake around the centre of each large serving plate. Randomly pipe little dots of mandarin gel around the cake and garnish these with candied mandarin peel. Place a neat quenelle of coffee cream on one piece of coffee cake and sprinkle with a tiny pinch of sea salt. Arrange three mandarin segments on the plate, then scatter coffee meringue pieces randomly. Finally, place a neat scoop or quenelle of ice cream on a coffee cake piece and serve immediately.

RESTAURANT DESSERTS

SOCIAL SWEETS

CHOCOLATE MOUSSE, HAZELNUT & BURNT ORANGE

This chocolate mousse recipe is from Esquina, our tapas bar in Singapore, and it is an easy and delectable dessert to make for a dinner party. When my chefs and I develop recipes, we are always careful to balance the flavours and textures of our dishes and desserts are no exception. For this, we cut the richness of the silky chocolate mousse with some burnt orange segments. A little chocolate soil and toasted, chopped hazelnuts provide textural contrast and a pinch of sea salt brings out the flavour of the dark chocolate. At the restaurant, we also serve the mousse with popcorn-infused milk but I've left this out here to keep things simple.

SERVES 8–10

For the chocolate mousse
150g dark chocolate (with 72% cocoa
    solids), chopped
190ml whole milk
7 medium egg yolks
40g caster sugar
190ml double cream

For the burnt orange
2–3 medium oranges
icing sugar, for dusting

To serve
Chocolate Soil (see page 242)
a handful of toasted hazelnuts
sea salt

To make the chocolate mousse, put the chopped chocolate into a heatproof bowl and set aside. Bring the milk to the boil in a small saucepan. As soon as the milk begins to bubble, pour it over the chocolate. Stir until the chocolate has melted and the mixture is smooth. Leave to cool completely, then cover the bowl with cling film and refrigerate for an hour.

Meanwhile, put the egg yolks and sugar in a large heatproof mixing bowl and beat with an electric whisk until the mixture is light and fluffy. Set the bowl over a pan of gently simmering water and whisk the mixture until it is pale and thick and has tripled in volume. Take the bowl off the pan and continue to whisk until the mixture has cooled slightly and the side of the bowl no longer feels hot. Set aside.

In another bowl, whip the cream to soft peaks. Using the same whisk, beat the cold chocolate mixture until it is aerated and will hold soft peaks. Fold the whipped chocolate into the egg mixture. When well combined, fold through the whipped cream, adding it in two or three batches. Transfer the mixture to a container, cover and chill for a few hours until set.

Shortly before serving, prepare the burnt orange. Peel the oranges and separate the segments, cutting them from the membrane. Arrange the segments in a single layer on a baking tray. Dust the segments with sifted icing sugar, then run a blowtorch over them until the sugar has caramelised and the segments are flecked with blackened bits.

To assemble the dessert, spoon a little chocolate soil into individual serving bowls and place a neat scoop or quenelle of chocolate mousse on top and sprinkle with a tiny pinch of sea salt. Garnish the mousse with burnt orange segments. Grate over some toasted hazelnuts (or sprinkle with crushed toasted hazelnuts). Serve immediately.

SCOTTISH RASPBERRY PAVLOVA WITH VANILLA CREAM AND RED WINE AND RASPBERRY GRANITA

This is playful and attractive take on the classic dessert named after the Russian ballerina, Anna Pavlova. It is an easy dessert to assemble and every component of the dish can be made a day or two in advance.

SERVES 5–6

For the raspberry and red wine granita
250g raspberries (thawed if frozen)
190g caster sugar
300ml water
375ml red wine

For the mascarpone cream
2 gelatine leaves
300ml double cream
50g caster sugar
1 vanilla pod, split in half, seeds scraped out with a knife
150g mascarpone

For the meringue discs
3 large egg whites
150g caster sugar
1 teaspoon cornflour
1 teaspoon white wine vinegar

For the raspberry jelly (optional)
200g raspberries (thawed if frozen)
50ml water
130g caster sugar
7g powdered pectin
½ teaspoon lime juice

To serve
400g fresh raspberries
Candied Mint (see page 241)

To make the granita, put the raspberries, sugar and water into a saucepan and stir over medium heat just until the sugar has dissolved. Take the pan off the heat and pour the raspberries and syrup into a blender. Blitz until smooth. Pass the mixture through a fine sieve into a bowl. Stir in the red wine. Pour into a freezerproof container, cover and freeze. The next day, scrape the frozen mixture with a fork to get flaky ice crystals, then keep in the freezer until ready to serve.

For the mascarpone cream, soak the gelatine leaves in a bowl of cold water for a few minutes to soften. Meanwhile, heat the cream with the sugar and vanilla seeds and pod in a pan, stirring to dissolve the sugar. Just before the cream starts to boil, take the pan off the heat. Squeeze out the excess water from the gelatine leaves, then add to the warm cream and stir until melted. Whisk in the mascarpone. Strain the mixture through a fine sieve into a baking tray or other wide container. Cool completely, then refrigerate overnight to set.

To make the meringue discs, preheat the oven to 120°C/Fan 100°C/Gas Mark ½. Line two baking sheets with silicone mats or baking parchment. Put the egg whites into the bowl of an electric mixer fitted with the whisk attachment. Whisk the whites on high speed to soft peaks. Reduce the speed slightly, then gradually add the sugar, a tablespoon at a time, whisking for 3–5 seconds between each addition. When all the sugar has been incorporated, continue to whisk until the meringue is stiff and glossy. Add the cornflour and vinegar and whisk for another minute.

Spoon the meringue into a piping bag fitted with a plain 1–1.25cm nozzle. If using baking parchment, secure it to the baking sheet with little dabs of meringue. Pipe 10–12 discs of meringue, each about the diameter of your fist, on the lined baking sheets. Dry out in the oven for 1½–2 hours or until the meringues feel firm and set on the outside (the centre will be like marshmallow) and you can easily lift them off the silicone mat or parchment. Leave to cool completely, then store in an airtight container until ready to serve.

For the raspberry jelly, put the raspberries and water into a pan and mash the raspberries with a fork. Bring to the boil. Meanwhile, stir the sugar and pectin together in a small bowl. As soon as the raspberry mixture begins to boil, turn the heat down and stir in the sugar mixture. Stir over medium heat for about 5 minutes or until the mixture thickens. Take the pan off the heat and whisk in the lime juice. Strain the mixture through a fine sieve into a small tray. Leave to cool completely, then cover with cling film and refrigerate for a few hours until set. For serving, cut into 1cm cubes.

To assemble the dessert, whisk the mascarpone cream to soft peaks, then spoon it into a piping bag fitted with a plain 1cm nozzle. Place a meringue disc on each serving plate, securing it to the plate with a dab of mascarpone cream, then pipe mascarpone cream on top of the meringue. Place several cubes of raspberry jelly on the cream and arrange fresh raspberries around this. Top with another meringue disc and garnish it with jelly, raspberries and candied mint. Serve the granita on the side.

COCONUT MERINGUE WITH MANGO SORBET, PINEAPPLE, COCONUT AND CURRY CRUMBLE

Being married to a Filipina and having spent much time in the Far East, I am partial to using Asian flavours and ingredients in my cooking. My wife, Irha, is from Cebu, which is considered to be the mango capital of the Philippines. This dessert is dedicated to her. The mango sorbet is delightfully refreshing and it marries so well with the coconut meringues, pineapple and curry crumble. The coconut and curry crumble may sound a little outlandish, but trust me, it works a treat. If you really don't like the taste of curry, leave it out.

SERVES 10–12

For the coconut meringues
2 large egg whites
150g caster sugar
100g coconut powder (or fine desiccated coconut), toasted
a pinch of fine sea salt

For the curry crumble
125g unsalted butter, softened
½ vanilla pod, split in half, seeds scraped out with a knife
30g icing sugar, sifted
125g plain flour
¼ teaspoon fine sea salt
½ tablespoon mild curry powder
15g coconut powder (or fine desiccated coconut)

For the calamansi gel
225ml calamansi juice (or fresh lime juice), strained
3g powdered pectin
5g agar agar powder
75g caster sugar

For the vanilla pineapple dice
½ small, ripe pineapple
100ml Vanilla Stock Syrup (see page 242)

For the mango carpaccio
1 large, firm but ripe mango

To serve
a handful of coriander cress (or picked baby coriander leaves)
a handful of toasted flaked coconut
1 kaffir lime, frozen
Mango and Lime Sorbet (see page 209)
Pineapple Crisps (see page 241)

First, make the coconut meringues. Preheat the oven to 120°C/Fan 100°C/Gas Mark ½, and line two baking sheets with silicone mats or baking parchment. (If using baking parchment, use a 10p coin as a guide to draw neat rows of circles on the parchment, leaving a 2–3cm gap between the circles; these will be a size guide for the meringues. Flip over the parchment sheets so that the pencil marks are underneath before lining the baking sheets.)

Lightly whisk together the egg whites and sugar in a large heatproof mixing bowl using an electric whisk. Set the bowl over a saucepan of gently simmering water and whisk the mixture at high speed for about 5 minutes to make a pale and glossy meringue. Take the bowl off the pan and continue to whisk the meringue for a few more minutes or until it has cooled and the base of the bowl no longer feels hot to the touch. Spoon the meringue into a large piping bag fitted with a 1–1.5cm plain nozzle.

Mix the coconut powder with a pinch of salt, then sprinkle a thin layer over the prepared baking sheets. Pipe tall mounds of meringue on top (within the drawn circles, if using baking parchment, or each about the diameter of a 10p coin if using silicone mats). Sprinkle the meringues with the remaining coconut powder. Dry out in the oven for 1½–2 hours or until the meringues are lightly coloured and firm. Remove from the oven and leave to cool. Keep in an airtight container until ready to serve.

Next, make the curry crumble. Turn the oven up to 150°C/Fan 130°C/Gas Mark 2. Line a large baking sheet with a silicone mat or baking parchment. Combine the butter, vanilla seeds and icing sugar in a large mixing bowl and stir together using a wooden spoon. Sift in the flour, salt and curry powder and add the coconut powder. Mix gently until the ingredients come together to make a soft dough.

Tip the dough on to the lined baking sheet and press out to a rough rectangle. Lay a sheet of baking parchment on top, then roll out the dough to the thickness of a £1 coin. Remove the top sheet of parchment, then bake for 20–25 minutes or until light golden brown. Leave to cool completely,

(continued on page 154)

then crumble the curry pastry with your hands. Keep in an airtight container until ready to serve.

To make the calamansi gel, put all the ingredients into a small saucepan and stir over medium-low heat until the sugar and agar agar have dissolved. Increase the heat and bring to the boil. Boil for a few minutes, then pour into a small bowl. Leave to cool completely. Once cold, cover the bowl with cling film and chill the mixture for a few hours until thickened.

To prepare the pineapple, cut off the skin, then cut the flesh into 1.5cm dice, discarding the hard core. Put the diced pineapple into a sealable bag and pour in the vanilla syrup. Press out as much air as possible, then seal the bag; ensure that the pineapple is evenly covered with the syrup. Macerate in the fridge for at least an hour or until ready to serve.

For the mango carpaccio, peel off the mango skin with a vegetable peeler, then cut away the two 'cheeks' of flesh from either side of the stone. Thinly slice the mango flesh. Lay the slices between pieces of greaseproof paper and keep in the fridge until ready to serve.

To assemble the dessert, place a little curry crumble on each serving plate and spoon a little calamansi gel over it. Top the gel with a few slices of mango carpaccio. Run a blowtorch over the tops of the coconut meringues to lightly toast them, then place four or five meringues around each plate. Dot the pineapple cubes around the plates and decorate them with a little coriander cress and toasted coconut flakes. Grate a little kaffir lime zest over each plate. Finally, add a neat scoop of sorbet to each plate and garnish with a pineapple crisp. Serve at once.

RESTAURANT DESSERTS

SOCIAL SWEETS

APPLE, BEETROOT AND CARROT ('ABC')

My pastry chef at Pollen Singapore came up with this unique dessert for those who do not have a sweet tooth. Apart from the ice cream, which holds all the components of the dish together, the dessert relies primarily on the natural sweetness of apples, beetroot and carrot.

SERVES 8

For the apple segments
1 large or 2 small eating apples
100ml beetroot juice

For the roasted beetroot purée
1 large red beetroot, about 200g
light olive oil, for drizzling

For the roasted yellow beetroot
4–6 yellow baby beetroots, about 350g

For the sautéed carrots
1 medium carrot, about 200g
1 tablespoon vegetable oil

For the pickled red beetroot
1 red beetroot, about 180g
50ml apple balsamic vinegar

For the apple sauce
25g caster sugar
75ml white wine
1 vanilla pod, split in half, seeds
 scraped out with a knife
2 green eating apples
sea salt and freshly ground black
 pepper

To serve
White Balsamic Ice Cream (see page
 180)

To prepare the apple segments, peel and core the apple, then cut into thin wedges. Place them in a resealable bag and pour in the beetroot juice. Seal tightly, squeezing out as much air as possible. Chill for at least 2 hours.

Next roast the yellow beetroots and the red beetroot for the beetroot purée. Preheat the oven to 180°C/Fan 160°C/Gas Mark 4. Place the unpeeled red beetroot on a piece of foil and drizzle over a light coating of oil, then season well with salt and pepper. Wrap up in the foil and place on a small roasting tray.

Peel the yellow beetroots and cut the flesh into 1cm slices. Stack up several slices at a time and stamp out neat discs with a 7.5cm pastry cutter. Place the discs in a bowl and toss with a pinch each of salt and pepper and a little oil. Wrap the seasoned beetroot slices in a large piece of foil and add to the roasting tray.

Place the tray in the oven. Roast the yellow beetroot slices for 30–40 minutes or until they are tender when pierced with the tip of a small, sharp knife. Take them out of the oven and leave to cool.

The whole red beetroot will take longer to cook – about an hour altogether. When ready, remove it from its foil wrapping and leave to cool slightly before peeling off the skin. Roughly chop the flesh, then place in a small food processor and blitz to a smooth purée. Transfer to a bowl and leave to cool before covering and keeping in the fridge. About 30 minutes before serving take the purée out of the fridge to come to room temperature.

For the sautéed carrots, peel the carrot and cut it into neat 1cm dice. Heat the oil in a wide frying pan, add the carrot dice with a pinch of salt and sauté over medium-low heat for 4–6 minutes or until just tender but not browned. Transfer to a plate and keep at room temperature.

For the pickled beetroot, peel the beetroot and slice very thinly using a mandoline. To make perfect circles, stack up several slices at a time and stamp out discs using a 5cm pastry cuttter. Place the discs in a resealable bag, add the vinegar and seal, pressing out all the air in the bag as you do so. Leave to pickle in the fridge for 2 hours.

To make the apple sauce, put the sugar, wine and vanilla pod and seeds into a heavy-based saucepan. Peel and core the apples, then roughly chop them. As you chop the apples, add them to the pan. Cook over medium heat for 15–20 minutes or until the apples are very soft and almost all of liquid has evaporated. While still hot, transfer the mixture to a small food processor and blitz on high speed to make a very smooth sauce. Strain the sauce through a sieve into a bowl and leave to cool. Cover and keep in the fridge until ready to use.

To assemble the dessert, place little teaspoonfuls of apple sauce randomly around each serving plate, then arrange a couple of discs of beetroot-marinated apple segments on top. Add two neat spoonfuls of beetroot purée to the plate, then place several discs of roasted yellow beetroot and pickled beetroot on top. Finally, place a spoonful of sautéed carrots on the plate and top it with a scoop of ice cream. Serve at once.

COCONUT PANNA COTTA, MANGO SORBET, RAW PEACH SALAD, CANDIED TARRAGON AND ORANGE BISCUIT

This is another dish that is consistently on our dessert menu at Esquina. It is a truly successful fusion of Asian and Western ingredients and techniques. I like to think of it as the perfect pudding for novice cooks, as it does not require much skill or experience to create a stunning dessert. Peaches have a short season so we often replace them with sweet cantaloupe or charantais melons at other times of the year.

SERVE 6–8

For the coconut panna cotta
3 gelatine leaves
400ml double cream
200ml whole milk
100g caster sugar
60ml coconut milk
25ml coconut liqueur (such as
    Malibu)

For the orange biscuit crumbs
250g plain flour
125g caster sugar
1 teaspoon fine sea salt
finely grated zest of 2 oranges
125g cold unsalted butter, diced

For the raw peach salad
3 ripe peaches
50ml Vanilla Stock Syrup (see page
    242)

To serve
Mango and Lime Sorbet (see page
    209)
Candied Tarragon (see page 241)

First prepare the panna cotta. Soak the gelatine sheets in a small bowl of cold water for a few minutes to soften. Meanwhile, put the cream, milk and sugar into a heavy-based saucepan and stir over medium heat until the sugar has dissolved. Bring the creamy milk to a simmer, then take pan off the heat. Squeeze out the excess water from the gelatine leaves, add to the pan and stir until melted. Stir in the coconut milk. Leave the mixture to cool completely before stirring in the coconut liqueur.

Pour the mixture into individual serving bowls. Carefully place the bowls in the fridge and leave for a few hours (or overnight) until set.

Next make the orange biscuit crumbs. Preheat the oven to 160°C/Fan 140°C/Gas Mark 3. Sift the flour, sugar and salt into the bowl of an electric mixer fitted with the paddle attachment. Stir in the orange zest. Add the diced butter and mix on low speed until the mixture has both large and small crumbs. Spread the mixture evenly on a baking tray. Bake for 20–25 minutes, stirring occasionally, until the crumbs are golden brown and crisp. Leave to cool completely, then store in an airtight container until ready to serve.

For the peach salad, cut the peaches in half and remove the stones, then slice thinly into rounds. Place in a bowl, add the vanilla syrup and toss gently to coat. Cover and set aside (the peaches can be prepared a few hours ahead).

To assemble, overlap five or six macerated peach slices on top of each panna cotta. Scatter a small handful of orange biscuit crumbs on top of the peach slices, then top with a neat scoop of sorbet. Garnish with a few pieces of candied tarragon and serve at once.

RESTAURANT DESSERTS

CHOCOLATE GANACHE WITH SEA SALT AND PISTACHIO PARFAIT

I got the idea for this dessert whilst watching my daughter, Keziah, tuck into a brioche toast slathered with Nutella one morning. But rather than making the brioche the star of the show, I'm emphasising the chocolate and nut elements with the dark chocolate ganache and pistachio parfait. The brioche croutons play a supporting role by adding crunch to the dessert.

SERVES 10

For the chocolate ganache
50g unsalted butter, diced
150g dark chocolate (with about 70% cocoa solids), chopped
60g caster sugar
2 tablespoons water
1 large egg
1 medium egg yolk
185ml double cream

For the pistachio parfait
110g caster sugar
80ml water
8 large egg yolks
60g pistachio paste
5 large egg whites
190ml double cream

For the brioche croutons
4 thick slices of Brioche Loaf (see page 24)
olive oil, for drizzling

To serve
Chocolate Soil (see page 242)
Maldon sea salt, for sprinkling

To make the chocolate ganache, put the butter and chocolate in a heatproof bowl and set the bowl over a pan of gently simmering water. Stir until melted and smooth. Take the bowl off the pan and set aside.

Next, make a pâte à bombe. Put the sugar and 50ml water in a small heavy-based pan and stir over medium heat until the sugar has dissolved. Increase the heat and place a sugar thermometer in the pan. Let the sugar syrup boil vigorously until it reaches 120°C. Meanwhile, beat the egg and egg yolk together in a large bowl using an electric whisk until the mixture is pale, light and tripled in volume. When the sugar syrup has reached the right temperature, very carefully trickle it over the beaten eggs, whisking constantly. Keep whisking until the mixture has cooled a little and the side of the bowl no longer feels hot.

Fold the melted chocolate through the pâte à bombe. Whip the cream to soft peaks, then fold into the chocolate pâte à bombe. Pour the mixture into a large container, cover and keep in the fridge until ready to serve.

For the pistachio parfait, line a large loaf tin with cling film and set aside. (You could also set the parfait in small moulds as we do at the restaurants; however, it does require a lot of freezer space.) Make a pâte à bombe with 55g of the sugar, 30ml (2 tablespoons) of the water and the egg yolks (as you have done for the chocolate ganache above), then fold through the pistachio paste.

Next, make an Italian meringue. Put the remaining sugar and water into a heavy-based saucepan and stir over medium heat to dissolve the sugar. Increase the heat and leave the sugar syrup to boil until it reaches 120°C. Meanwhile, wash the beaters of the whisk well and dry them, then use to whisk the egg whites in a large bowl to stiff peaks. When the sugar syrup is ready, gradually trickle it over the egg whites, whisking constantly. When fully incorporated, carry on whisking the meringue until it cools and the side of the bowl no longer feels hot.

In another bowl, whip the cream to soft peaks. Fold the cream into the pistachio mixture followed by the Italian meringue. Pour the parfait mixture into the prepared tin and spread evenly. Cover with cling film and freeze for about 4 hours or until set.

For the brioche croutons, preheat the oven to 180°C/Fan 160°C/Gas Mark 4. Cut the brioche slices into 2cm cubes and place them in a large bowl. Drizzle over a little olive oil and toss until all the cubes are lightly coated. Spread the croutons in a single layer on a large baking sheet and bake for 10–15 minutes, turning once, until they are evenly golden brown and crisp. Leave to cool completely before storing in an airtight container.

When you are ready to assemble the dessert, unmould the pistachio parfait on to a cutting board and cut into neat slices. Place a slice on each serving plate. Add a few neat spoonfuls or quenelles of chocolate ganache alongside. Sprinkle the chocolate ganache with chocolate soil and a little pinch of Maldon sea salt. Finally, scatter the brioche croutons around and serve at once.

PEANUT PARFAIT, RED FRUIT AND SALTED PEANUT CARAMEL

This is a scrumptious take on my signature Peanut Butter and Jelly (PBJ) dessert from Maze. It is packed with the rich flavour of peanuts in a variety of textures, which is all nicely offset by the fresh berries and cherry sorbet. If you are short of time, leave out the peanut bricelet and replace the peanut crunch with a sprinkling of chopped salted and roasted peanuts.

SERVES 10

For the peanut parfait
225g smooth peanut butter
525ml double cream
75ml Frangelico
3 large eggs
3 large egg yolks
225g caster sugar
6 large egg whites

For the peanut bricelet
120g caster sugar
½ teaspoon powdered pectin
100g unsalted butter
40ml double cream
40g liquid glucose
2g Maldon sea salt
140g blanched peanuts, roughly ground in a food processor

For the peanut crunch
200g white chocolate, roughly chopped
130g smooth peanut butter
150g *pailletté feuilletine* (or finely crushed cornflakes)

To serve
Raspberry Jam (see page 245)
Cherry Sorbet (see page 196)
200g mixed soft fruit, such as raspberries, redcurrants and blueberries
100g frozen raspberries

It is best to make the peanut parfait the day before you intend to serve it. Half fill a pan with water and bring to a simmer. Put the peanut butter, 150ml double cream and the Frangelico into a large mixing bowl and whisk until smooth; set aside.

In another mixing bowl that is heatproof, combine the eggs, egg yolks and 150g of the sugar and beat with an electric whisk until pale and fluffy. When the water in the pan is gently simmering, set the heatproof bowl on top and whisk the egg mixture for a few minutes until it is thick and glossy. Take the bowl off the pan and continue to whisk until the mixture has cooled slightly. Set aside.

Put the remaining 75g of sugar into a small heavy-based saucepan with a splash of water. Stir over low heat until the sugar has dissolved, then increase the heat to high and let the sugar syrup boil until it reaches 120°C on a sugar thermometer. Meanwhile, wash the beaters of the electric whisk well to make sure they are grease-free and dry them, then whisk the egg whites in a large mixing bowl to stiff peaks. When the sugar syrup has reached the right temperature, slowly trickle it on to the egg whites, whisking constantly as you do so. Continue to whisk the meringue until it has cooled slightly.

Use the same whisk to whip the remaining 375ml of double cream in another bowl to soft peaks. Fold this through the peanut butter base followed by the egg yolk mixture and finally the meringue.

Line a shallow 2 litre freezerproof container or a large loaf tin with cling film. (At the restaurant we use thin cylindrical moulds for individual parfaits but at home it is easier to set the mixture in a large container, then slice to serve.) Pour the peanut parfait into the container, cover and freeze overnight until set.

To make the peanut bricelet, stir together the sugar and pectin, then tip the mixture into a heavy-based pan. Add the butter, cream, liquid glucose and salt. Set the pan over medium heat and stir until the mixture is smooth. Just before the mixture begins to boil, take the pan off the heat and stir in the ground peanuts.

Spread the mixture out on a silicone mat. Lay a sheet of greaseproof paper on top and roll out the mixture thinly. Slide the mat on to a large baking sheet and chill for at least 30 minutes or until firm.

Preheat the oven to 160°C/Fan 140°C/ Gas Mark 3. Remove the greaseproof paper and bake the peanut bricelet for 10–15 minutes or until golden brown and crisp. Leave to cool slightly. While it is still warm and pliable, cut the bricelet with a long sharp knife into strips about 2 x 9cm. If the bricelet has cooled too much and is too brittle to cut, pop it back into the oven for a few minutes until it has softened and is once again pliable. Cool completely before storing the bricelet strips in between

sheets of greaseproof paper in an airtight container.

To make the peanut crunch, put the white chocolate in a heatproof bowl, set the bowl over a pan of gently simmering water and stir the chocolate until just softened. Take the bowl off the pan and stir the chocolate until smooth, then stir in the peanut butter followed by the *feuilletine*. Drop small teaspoonfuls of the peanut crunch on a

baking sheet lined with a silicone mat. Chill for at least 30 minutes or until set. Once set, transfer to an airtight container and keep at room temperature until needed.

When you are ready to serve the dessert, unmould and unwrap the peanut parfait, then use a warmed knife to cut it into 2cm slices. If you wish, you can cut each slice into long strips about the same size as the peanut bricelets. Place two strips of peanut

bricelet on each serving plate and top with the peanut parfait. Dot or pipe little mounds of raspberry jam around the plate, then scatter over the peanut crunch. Place a neat scoop or quenelle of sorbet next to the parfait. Working quickly, add a handful of mixed soft fruit to the plate, then lightly crush the frozen raspberries and scatter the raspberry seeds around the plate. Serve at once.

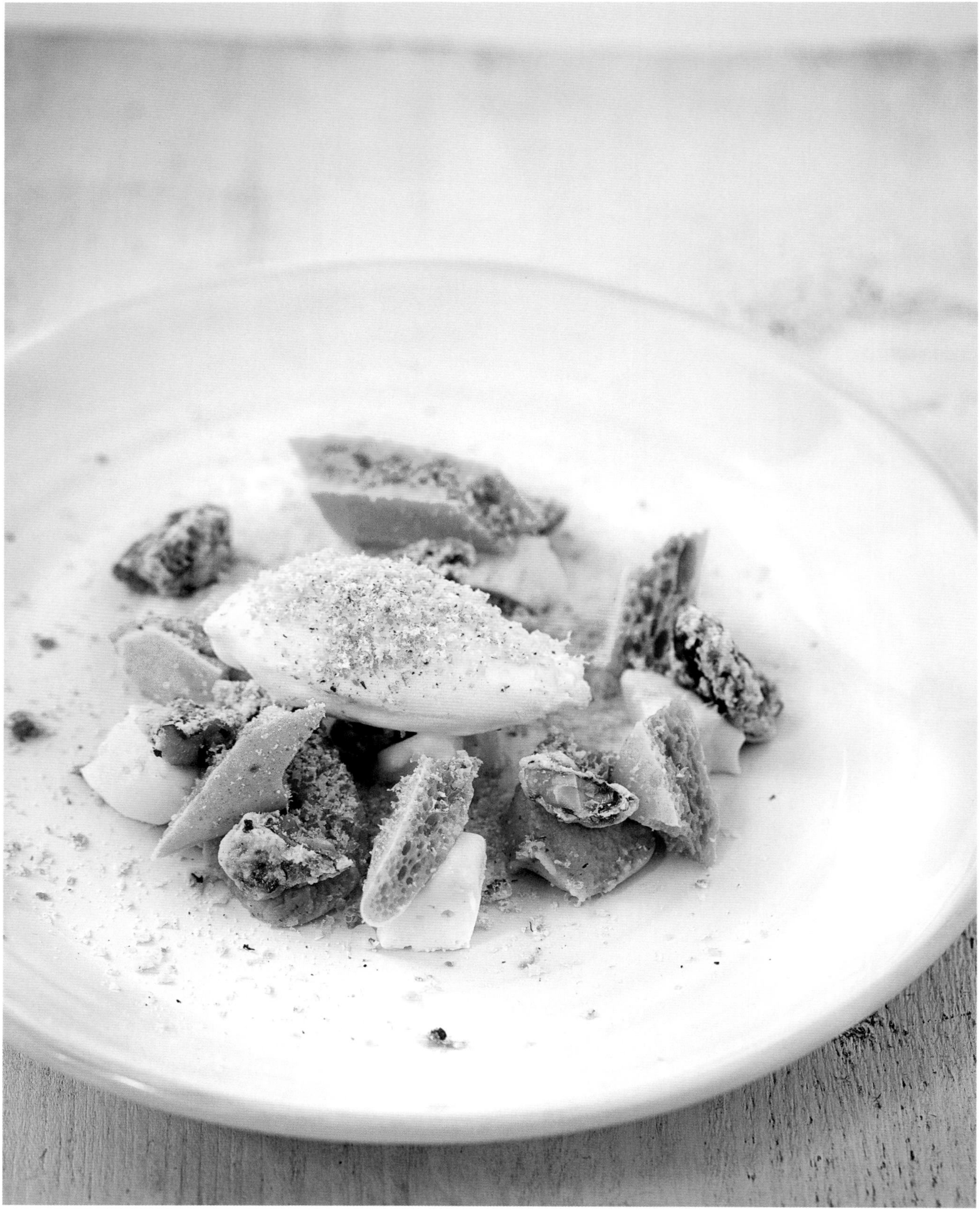

GOAT'S CHEESE, FROMAGE FRAIS SORBET, HONEYCOMB AND SWEET WALNUTS

I learnt to make fromage frais sorbet back in 1988 when I first embarked on my cooking career. Back then, I thought it was so inventive to use a creamy cheese to flavour a sorbet. Now the sorbet has become one of my staple recipes and we almost always have it in the restaurant freezers to accompany a host of desserts. Here, the fromage frais sorbet is teamed with goat's cheese and walnuts, a combination that is more commonly seen in savoury starters. It is certainly a dessert for the adventurous.

SERVES 10

For the walnut jelly
200g toasted walnuts (see below)
40ml vegetable oil
250g white chocolate chips
7g agar agar powder
25g caster sugar
9g powdered pectin
800ml water

For the sweet walnuts
250g toasted walnuts (see below)
100g caster sugar
25ml water

To serve
2–3 toasted walnuts, for grating
250g soft crumbly goat's cheese, cut
    into cubes
honeycomb (see Chocolate-coated
    Honeycomb on page 49), broken
    into small shards
Fromage Frais Sorbet (see page 208)

To toast the walnuts for the jelly, sweet walnuts and garnish, preheat the oven to 160°C/Fan 140°C/Gas Mark 3. Spread out all the walnuts (about 500g) on a baking sheet and toast in the oven for 5–6 minutes. Leave to cool.

For the walnut jelly, line a small baking tray with cling film. Put the 200g toasted walnuts and the oil into a food processor and blitz for a few minutes to a smooth, wet paste. (You need to process the nuts until they begin to release their oil.) Scrape the paste into a large mixing bowl. Add the white chocolate chips and set aside.

Mix together the agar agar, sugar, pectin and water in a saucepan. Stir over medium-low heat until the liquid is clear, then increase the heat and bring to a simmer. As soon as the syrup begins to simmer, pour it over the chocolate chips and walnut paste. Stir until the chocolate has melted and the mixture is smooth. Pour into the lined baking tray and spread out evenly to about 2cm thickness. Leave to cool, then chill for a couple of hours until set. Cut the walnut jelly into neat squares for serving.

For the sweet walnuts, put the sugar and water into a large pan and set over medium heat. Without stirring, let the sugar dissolve and the syrup come to a simmer. Remove from the heat, then tip in the 250g toasted walnuts and mix with a wooden spoon until the nuts are well coated with the sugar syrup. Keep stirring until the nuts begin to look like they're covered with a white sugar coating. Spread the nuts on a baking sheet and leave to cool completely. Keep in an airtight container until ready to serve.

To assemble the dessert, arrange some cubes of walnut jelly and goat's cheese around each serving plate, leaving space in the centre for the sorbet. Garnish the jelly with the sweet walnuts and stick some honeycomb pieces on the goat's cheese cubes. Add a neat scoop of sorbet to the centre of the plate, then grate some toasted walnut over it. Serve at once.

HOT CHOCOLATE MOELLEUX WITH SEA SALT AND ALMOND ICE CREAM

This was one of the first desserts I created at Maze and because it is so good, we're still serving it at Little Social today. I came up with it as a way to serve large amounts of chocolate fondants, which were all the rage at the time, in a consistent manner. By baking the chocolate mixture in beautiful little china cups, we were able to serve 260 portions of chocolate moelleux a day. The warm chocolate moelleux teamed with cold salted almond ice cream is just sublime and this has become one of our classics.

SERVES 8

For the cardamom caramel
2 cardamom pods, lightly crushed
100ml double cream
100g caster sugar

For the hot chocolate moelleux
135g dark chocolate (with 70% cocoa solids), chopped
135g unsalted butter, plus extra for greasing
4 large egg whites
5 large egg yolks
180g caster sugar
60g plain flour, sifted

To serve
Sea Salt and Almond Ice Cream (see page 185)

First, prepare the cardamom caramel. Put the cardamom and cream in a saucepan and slowly bring to a simmer. Meanwhile, put the sugar into another heavy-based pan and heat until the sugar begins to melt around the edges. Tilt the pan from side to side to encourage the sugar to melt evenly, then let it caramelise to an amber colour. Take the pan off the heat and carefully pour in the cardamom-infused milk. If any caramel hardens upon contact with the milk, return the pan to low heat and stir until melted. Strain the caramel sauce through a fine sieve into a jug and discard the cardamom. Once cooled, transfer to a squeezy bottle.

For the hot chocolate moelleux, put the chocolate and butter into a heatproof bowl and set over a pan of gently simmering water. Stir occasionally until melted and smooth. Take the bowl off the pan and set aside.

Preheat the oven to 190°C/Fan 170°C/ Gas Mark 5. Generously butter eight 150ml ramekins or individual ovenproof bowls, then set them on a wide baking tray. Put the egg whites in a clean mixing bowl and combine the egg yolks and sugar in another bowl. Use an electric whisk to beat the egg whites to soft peaks. Using the same beaters, whisk the egg yolks with the sugar until the mixture is light and fluffy. Add the melted chocolate to the yolk mixture and fold through, then add the sifted flour and fold again. Finally, fold in the egg whites until well combined.

Spoon enough of the mixture into the prepared ramekins or bowls to half fill them. Squeeze a little cardamom caramel into the middle of each one, then cover with a little more chocolate mixture until the ramekins or bowls are three quarters full. Bake for 8–10 minutes or until the cakes are set around the edges but still moist and runny in the centre – the surface should look set but have a slight wobble. Let them cool for a minute before serving with a scoop of ice cream alongside each one.

RESTAURANT DESSERTS

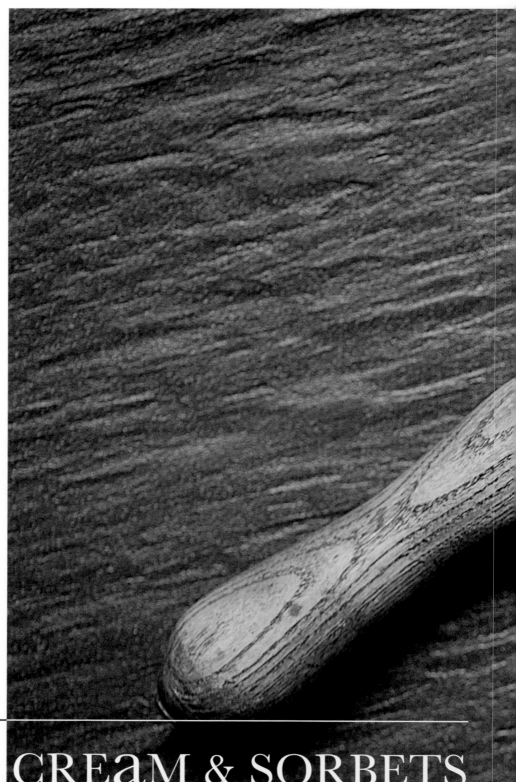

ICE CREAM & SORBETS

ICE CREAM & SORBETS

193/ LYCHEE SORBET 194/ CREAM CHEESE AND LIME SORBET 195/ CUCUMBER SORBET
196/ CHERRY SORBET 198/ COCONUT AND MALIBU SORBET 199/ STRAWBERRY AND
HIBISCUS SORBET 201/ CHOCOLATE SORBET 202/ STRAWBERRY SAKE SORBET
203/ PEACH SORBET 204/ PASSION FRUIT SORBET 207/ RASPBERRY AND YUZU SORBET
208/ FROMAGE FRAIS (OR YOGHURT) SORBET 209/ MANGO AND LIME SORBET
210/ VERBENA AND OLIVE OIL SORBET 213/ GREEN BASIL SORBET

A GENERAL NOTE ABOUT CHURNING ICE CREAMS AND SORBETS

Using an ice-cream machine is the best way to make ice creams and sorbets. The simultaneous cooling and churning process of the machine produces ice creams and sorbets with very fine ice crystals that feel smooth and creamy in the mouth. However, you can still make delicious ice creams and sorbets without a machine.

One alternative method is to freeze the base mixture in a shallow tray. Once it is solid, cut it into cubes or large pieces, quickly transfer to a strong blender or food processor and blitz to a smooth purée. Immediately pour this back into the container, cover and return to the freezer – you need to work swiftly to avoid the mixture melting. If you find that the result is still a little granular in texture, blend the ice cream or sorbet once more when it is solid again.

Another method is to freeze the ice cream or sorbet mixture in a wide container. After 1–1½ hours, when the mixture is not yet completely frozen, use a fork to stir the ice crystals from around the edges into the still liquid centre. Freeze for another hour, then stir the mixture again. Repeat the process three to four times until the mixture is frozen and solid. This method will create a coarser ice cream or sorbet.

Ice creams can be kept for a few months in the freezer but they tend to get icy with time. You can melt them down and re-churn them but custard-based ice creams won't re-freeze as well. Best to enjoy within a week or two. Take ice cream out of the freezer about 5 minutes before serving so it can soften a bit.

ICE CREAM & SORBETS

VANILLA ICE CREAM

MAKES ABOUT 700G

250ml double cream
250ml whole milk
1 vanilla pod, split in half, seeds
    scraped out with a knife
100g caster sugar
6 large egg yolks

Pour the cream and milk into a pan. Add both the vanilla seeds and pod and bring to the boil.

Meanwhile, whisk together the sugar and yolks in a bowl. As soon as the creamy milk bubbles up the side of the pan, remove from the heat and slowly trickle the liquid on to the sugary yolks, beating well. When all has been incorporated, pour the mixture into a clean heavy-based pan and stir over low-to-medium heat until the mixture thickens and will coat the back of the spoon. Leave to cool completely, stirring occasionally, then pass through a fine sieve.

Pour into the bowl of an ice-cream machine and churn until the ice cream is softly set. Transfer it to a freezerproof container, cover and freeze for a few hours or overnight until firm.

MASCARPONE AND PECAN ICE CREAM

MAKES ABOUT 1.1 LITRES

500g mascarpone
100g fromage frais
100g natural yoghurt
2 vanilla pods, split open, seeds
  scraped out with a knife
150g icing sugar, sifted
150ml whole milk
80g toasted pecans, lightly crushed

In a large bowl, mix together the mascarpone, fromage frais, yoghurt and vanilla seeds. Stir the icing sugar into the milk until it has dissolved, then gradually stir the sweetened milk into the mascarpone mixture. Use a stick blender to blitz the mixture until it is smooth.

Transfer the mixture to the bowl of an ice-cream machine and churn until softly set. Scrape the ice cream into a freezerproof container, then fold through the crushed pecans. Cover the container and freeze for several hours or overnight until firm.

VIN SANTO ICE CREAM

MAKES ABOUT 1.5 LITRES

500ml whole milk
500ml double cream
180g liquid glucose
8 large egg yolks
100g caster sugar
110ml vin santo

Put the milk, cream and liquid glucose into a saucepan and slowly bring to the boil. In the meantime, beat the yolks and sugar together in a bowl. When the creamy milk begins to bubble, remove from the heat and slowly trickle it into the egg mixture, stirring constantly. When fully incorporated, pour the mixture back into the pan. Stir over medium heat until thickened to a light custard that will thinly coat the spoon.

Strain the custard through a fine sieve into a wide bowl, then stir in the vin santo. Leave to cool, stirring occasionally to prevent a skin from forming.

When cold, pour the mixture into the bowl of an ice-cream machine and churn until softly set. Scrape the ice cream into a freezerproof container, cover and freeze for at least 4 hours or overnight until firm.

CLOTTED CREAM ICE CREAM

MAKES ABOUT 1 LITRE

670ml whole milk
100g caster sugar
30g liquid glucose
5 medium egg yolks
100g clotted cream

Put the milk into a heavy-based saucepan, along with the sugar and liquid glucose. Stir over a low heat to dissolve the sugar. Meanwhile, put the egg yolks into a large bowl and beat lightly. Once the sugar has dissolved, take the pan off the heat. Slowly add the warm milk to the eggs, whisking continuously as you do so.

Once everything is combined, return the mixture to the pan and stir over a low heat until the custard begins to thicken. When it's ready the custard should lightly coat the back of a spoon and you should be able to draw a line across it. Transfer the custard to a large bowl and leave to cool completely. Give it a stir every once in a while to prevent a skin from forming as it cools. Once cool, whisk in the clotted cream, using a beater or hand blender. Cover with cling film and chill for a few hours.

Pour the cold custard into the bowl of an ice-cream machine and churn until it has thickened and is beginning to set. Transfer to an airtight container and freeze for at least 2 hours or until the ice cream is firm. (If you don't have an ice-cream machine, freeze the custard in a suitable container for 90 minutes then stir the ice crystals with a fork to break them down. Freeze again and repeat the process 2 or 3 more times.)

ICE CREAM & SORBETS

WHITE BALSAMIC ICE CREAM

MAKES ABOUT 1 LITRE

480ml whole milk
120ml double cream
10g liquid glucose
5 large egg yolks
130g caster sugar
80ml white balsamic vinegar

Put the milk, cream and liquid glucose in a heavy-based saucepan over medium heat and bring to a simmer. Meanwhile, beat the egg yolks and sugar together in a large bowl. As soon as bubbles start to appear around the edge of the creamy milk, slowly trickle it over the yolk mixture, whisking constantly.

When fully incorporated, pour the mixture back into the pan and stir over medium heat until thickened to a light custard that will just coat the spoon. Strain the custard through a fine sieve into a wide bowl and leave to cool, stirring occasionally to prevent a skin from forming.

Once the custard has cooled, stir in the balsamic vinegar. Pour the mixture into the bowl of an ice-cream machine and churn until softly set. Scrape the ice cream into a freezerproof container, cover and freeze overnight until firm.

VANILLA AND PECAN ICE CREAM

MAKES ABOUT 1.5 LITRES

500ml double cream
500ml whole milk
2 vanilla pods, split in half, seeds
   scraped out with a knife
10 large egg yolks
200g caster sugar
80g roasted pecans, roughly chopped

Pour the cream and milk into a saucepan and add the vanilla pods and seeds. Bring to a simmer. Meanwhile, whisk the egg yolks and sugar together in a large bowl. When the creamy milk begins to bubble, slowly trickle it over the sugary eggs, whisking constantly. Once all the milk has been incorporated, strain the mixture through a fine sieve into a clean pan.

Stir over medium heat until thickened to a light custard that will coat the back of the spoon. Pour the custard into a wide bowl and leave to cool, stirring every once in a while to prevent a skin from forming.

When cold, pour the custard into the bowl of an ice-cream machine and churn until softly set. Add the chopped pecans and mix well. Transfer the ice cream to a freezerproof container, seal and freeze for several hours or until firm.

SOCIAL SWEETS

PUFF PASTRY ICE CREAM

This unusual ice cream is utterly delicious. At Little Social, we balance its buttery richness with fresh and zingy fruit such as peaches and raspberries (see page 127).

MAKES ABOUT 800ML

500g butter puff pastry (store-bought or see page 238 for a recipe)
1.5 litres whole milk
100g icing sugar, sifted
100ml double cream

Preheat the oven to 210°C/Fan 190°C/Gas Mark 7. On a lightly floured surface, roll out the puff pastry thinly, then place it on a large baking sheet. (If you'd like to serve the ice cream with some pieces of puff pastry, lightly score the pastry with your desired shapes now.) Bake the pastry for 25–30 minutes or until it is golden brown and crisp. Remove from the oven and leave to cool completely.

If you have marked out pastry shapes, cut them out and store in an airtight container until ready to serve. Break the remaining pastry into small pieces and place in a large bowl. Pour the milk over the broken pastry pieces and push down the pastry with a wooden spoon to ensure that it is all immersed. Cover with cling film and refrigerate overnight so the milk can become infused with the flavour of the puff pastry.

The next day, strain the milk through a fine sieve, pressing down on the soggy pastry with a wooden spoon to extract as much infused milk as possible. (This will require a bit of elbow grease.) You want to end up with about 500ml of infused milk. Add the icing sugar and cream to the milk and stir until the sugar has dissolved.

Pour the mixture into the bowl of an ice-cream machine and churn until softly set. Transfer the mixture to a freezerproof container, cover and freeze for 4 hours or overnight until firm.

YEAST ICE CREAM

Make the yeast ice cream two days before you intend to serve it.

MAKES ABOUT 1.35 LITRES

750ml whole milk
210ml double cream
125g liquid glucose
85g caster sugar
65g milk powder
6 medium egg yolks
6g powdered beer yeast

Put the milk, cream and liquid glucose into a saucepan and bring to a simmer. Meanwhile, stir together the sugar, milk powder and egg yolks in a mixing bowl. When the creamy milk begins to bubble, slowly stir it into the yolk mixture.

Pour the mixture back into the saucepan and stir over low-to-medium heat until thickened to a light custard that will just coat the spoon. Transfer to a bowl and leave to cool to about 35°C (or room temperature), giving the mixture a stir every once in a while to prevent a skin from forming.

Pour the cooled mixture into a container, add the beer yeast and stir well. Cover and chill for 12 hours or overnight. While the mixture is in the fridge, the yeast will become activated and the mixture will end up looking slightly split with lumpy curds and a watery layer beneath.

Give the mixture a stir, then pour it into the bowl of an ice-cream machine. Churn until the ice cream is softly set. Transfer to a freezerproof container, cover and freeze overnight or until firm.

SEA SALT AND ALMOND ICE CREAM

MAKES ABOUT 1.3 LITRES

800ml whole milk
40g liquid glucose
9g (scant 2 teaspoons) fine sea salt
140g caster sugar
6 medium egg yolks
160g toasted flaked almonds

Put the milk, liquid glucose and salt into a heavy-based saucepan and stir over a medium-to-low heat until the liquid glucose has dissolved. Slowly bring to a simmer. Meanwhile, stir together the sugar and egg yolks in a large bowl. When the milk begins to bubble, gradually pour it on to the sugary eggs, stirring constantly. Once all the milk has been incorporated, pour the mixture back into the pan and return to medium heat. Stir until thickened to a custard that will lightly coat the spoon.

Pour the custard into a wide bowl and add the toasted almonds. Leave to cool, giving the mixture an occasional stir to prevent a skin from forming.

When cold, strain the custard through a fine sieve into the bowl of an ice-cream machine. Churn until softly set, then transfer to a freezerproof container and cover. Freeze for a few hours or overnight until firm.

SALTED CARAMEL ICE CREAM

MAKES ABOUT 1 LITRE

470ml whole milk
210ml whipping cream
7 large egg yolks
180g caster sugar
½ teaspoon fine sea salt

Pour the milk and 70ml of the cream into a heavy-based saucepan and bring to a simmer. Meanwhile, beat the egg yolks with 3 tablespoons of the sugar in a bowl. When the creamy milk begins to bubble around the side of the pan, remove from the heat and slowly trickle on to the sugary yolks, whisking constantly.

Pour the mixture back into the saucepan. Add the salt, then stir with a wooden spoon over medium heat until the mixture thickens to a custard that will lightly coat the back of the spoon. Strain the custard through a fine sieve into a wide bowl. Leave to cool completely, stirring every so often to prevent a skin from forming.

Meanwhile, tip the remaining sugar into a heavy-based pan and place over high heat. Heat the remaining cream in a small saucepan. When the sugar begins to melt and caramelise around the edges, tilt the pan from side to side to encourage the sugar to melt and caramelise evenly. Once the caramel is golden brown, take the pan off the heat. Carefully pour in the warm cream, standing back as the hot caramel will spit and splutter as soon as it comes into contact with the cream, and swirl to mix together. If there are any bits of hardened caramel, return the pan to the heat and stir until the caramel sauce is smooth. Leave to cool, then strain the sauce through a fine sieve into the bowl containing the custard. Stir to mix well.

Pour the mixture into the bowl of an ice-cream machine and churn until softly set. Scrape the ice cream into a freezerproof container, cover and freeze for a few hours or overnight until firm.

ICE CREAM & SORBETS

ROASTED MANDARIN ICE CREAM

MAKES ABOUT 900ML

3 mandarin oranges
530ml whole milk
170ml double cream
20g liquid glucose
5 medium egg yolks
135g caster sugar
50g milk powder

Preheat the oven to 180°C/Fan 160°C/Gas Mark 4. Cut the mandarin oranges in half and place them, cut side down, on a baking sheet lined with baking parchment. Roast the oranges for 1–1½ hours or until the skins start to blacken. During roasting, the oranges will release their juices; carefully pour these off and return the skins to the oven to roast until they are ready.

Transfer the mandarin skins to a pan and pour in the milk. Bring to the boil, then immediately pour the milk and skins into a blender. Hold a kitchen towel over the lid of the blender and blitz the mixture for a couple of minutes or until the mandarin skins are well puréed. Strain the mixture through a fine sieve into a clean pan and discard the pulp.

Stir the cream and liquid glucose into the flavoured milk and bring to a simmer. Meanwhile, whisk the egg yolks, sugar and milk powder together in a large bowl. When the creamy orange milk starts to bubble, gradually whisk it into the yolk mixture. Pour back into the pan and stir over medium heat until thickened to a custard that will coat the spoon. Strain the custard through a fine sieve into a wide bowl and leave to cool, stirring every once in a while to prevent a skin from forming.

When cold, pour the custard into the bowl of an ice-cream machine and churn until softly set. Scrape the ice cream into a freezerproof container, cover and freeze for at least 4 hours or until firm.

LOVAGE ICE CREAM

Make the lovage ice cream a day ahead to allow it time to set.

MAKES ABOUT 1.4 LITRES

2 large bunches of lovage
1 teaspoon bicarbonate of soda
pinch of sea salt
60ml light olive or vegetable oil
750ml whole milk
345ml double cream
180g caster sugar
90g liquid glucose

Separate the leaves and stems of the lovage and set aside. Bring a medium saucepan of water to the boil and have ready a bowl of iced water. Add the bicarbonate of soda and salt to the boiling water and stir, then tip in the lovage leaves. Bring the water back to a simmer, then blanch the leaves for a couple of minutes. Drain the leaves and immediately plunge them into the iced water to cool them down quickly. Drain again, lightly squeezing out any excess water, then pat the blanched leaves dry with kitchen paper.

Put the leaves into a blender or small food processor and add the oil. Blitz for a minute or so to make a smooth green paste. Tip the paste into a muslin-lined sieve set over a bowl and leave the lovage-flavoured oil to drip through for 1–2 hours.

Meanwhile, roughly chop the lovage stems and put them into a saucepan. Add the milk, cream, sugar and liquid glucose. Gently heat the mixture until it begins to simmer, then remove from the heat and leave to cool and infuse for a few hours.

Strain the creamy mixture through a fine sieve into the bowl of an ice-cream machine. Add the lovage-infused oil and stir well. Churn the ice cream until it is softly set. Scrape into a freezerproof container, cover and freeze overnight until firm.

CHOCOLATE ICE CREAM

MAKES ABOUT 1.4 LITRES

750ml whole milk
2 tablespoons liquid glucose
200g dark chocolate (with about 70% cocoa solids), chopped
25g milk powder
185g caster sugar
200ml double cream
25ml chocolate liqueur (such as crème de cacao)

Pour the milk into a pan and add the liquid glucose. Set the pan on a medium heat and slowly bring to a simmer. Meanwhile, put the chopped chocolate into a large heatproof bowl. Mix the milk powder and sugar together, then add to the milk and give the mixture a stir to dissolve the sugar. Once the milk mixture is starting to simmer, pour it over the chopped chocolate. Use a stick blender to blitz together until smooth. Add the cream and chocolate liqueur and blitz again just to mix.

Leave the mixture to cool completely before pouring into the bowl of an ice-cream machine. Churn until the ice cream is softly set, then transfer to a freezerproof container. Cover and freeze for at least 4 hours or overnight until firm.

RUM AND RAISIN ICE CREAM

MAKES ABOUT 1.5 LITRES

500ml whole milk
500ml double cream
10 large egg yolks
200g caster sugar
75g liquid glucose
100g raisins, soaked overnight in 6
   tablespoons dark rum

Gently heat the milk and cream in a pan set over medium heat. In a large bowl, stir together the egg yolks, sugar and liquid glucose. When the creamy milk begins to simmer, slowly trickle it over the yolk mixture, stirring constantly. When fully incorporated, pour the mixture back into the pan and stir over medium heat until it thickens to a custard that will lightly coat the back of the spoon. Pour the custard through a fine sieve into a large bowl and leave to cool completely, stirring occasionally to prevent a skin from forming on top.

Once cooled, pour the custard into the bowl of an ice-cream machine and churn until softly set. Add the rum-soaked raisins and churn for another minute or two. Scrape the ice cream into a freezerproof container, cover and freeze for at least 4 hours or overnight until firm.

SOCIAL SWEETS

LYCHEE SORBET

MAKES ABOUT 850ML

2 x 400g cans lychees in syrup
50g liquid glucose

Tip the lychees and their syrup into a blender and add the liquid glucose. Blitz until the lychees are finely puréed. If your blender is not large enough, do this in two batches.

For a very smooth sorbet, pass the purée through a fine sieve, then pour into the bowl of an ice-cream machine. Churn until the sorbet is softly set. Transfer to a freezerproof container, cover and freeze for at least 4 hours or overnight until firm.

CREAM CHEESE AND LIME SORBET

MAKES ABOUT 1.2 LITRES

225g liquid glucose
225g caster sugar
500ml water
290g fromage frais
finely grated zest and juice of 5 limes

Put the liquid glucose, sugar and water into a heavy-based saucepan and stir over medium heat until the sugar has dissolved. Remove from the heat, then stir in the fromage frais and lime juice. Strain the mixture through a fine sieve into a large bowl. Add the lime zest and mix well, then leave to cool.

Once the mixture is cold, transfer it to the bowl of an ice-cream machine and churn until softly set. Scrape the sorbet into a freezerproof container, cover and freeze for several hours until firm.

CUCUMBER SORBET

MAKES ABOUT 1.2 LITRES

3 large cucumbers
300ml Stock Syrup (see page 242)
juice of 3 lemons
90ml Noilly Prat or other dry
   vermouth

Peel the cucumbers. Cut them lengthways
in half, then scoop out the seeds with a
spoon. Roughly chop the cucumber flesh.
Place it in a blender or food processor and
add the rest of the ingredients. Blitz until
very smooth.

Pass the sorbet mixture through a fine sieve
into the bowl of an ice-cream machine,
pressing down on the pulp with the back of
a spoon to extract as much juice as possible.
Churn until softly set. Scrape the sorbet
into a freezerproof container and freeze for
at least 4 hours or overnight until firm.

CHERRY SORBET

This homemade sorbet is quite thick as you end up with quite a bit of pulp in the mixture if you blend fresh cherries yourself. If you don't push the pulp through, you end up with very little sorbet.

MAKES 1–1.2 LITRES

50g caster sugar
50g liquid glucose
100ml water
2kg pitted fresh or frozen cherries
    (thawed if frozen)

Put the sugar, liquid glucose and water into a saucepan and stir over a medium-high heat until the sugar has dissolved. Add the cherries and simmer for about 5 minutes or until they are just soft but still retain their vivid colour. Carefully tip the cherries and poaching syrup into a blender and blitz until the cherries are well puréed.

Pass the cherry purée through a fine sieve into a wide bowl, pushing down on the pulp to get as much juice as possible. Discard the pulp. Leave to cool.

Transfer the cherry juice to the bowl of an ice-cream machine and churn until the sorbet is softly set. Scrape the sorbet into a freezerproof container, cover and freeze for several hours until firm.

ICE CREAM & SORBETS

COCONUT AND MALIBU SORBET

At the restaurants, we make this sorbet using Boiron coconut purée, which is a mixture of coconut milk and coconut juice. As Boiron purées are difficult to source, I have simplified the recipe to use coconut milk.

MAKES ABOUT 1 LITRE

75ml Malibu
160g liquid glucose
800ml (2 x 400g cans) coconut milk

Put the Malibu and liquid glucose into a saucepan and stir over gentle heat until the glucose has liquefied and mixed with the Malibu. Remove from the heat and pour in the coconut milk. Stir well, then leave to cool completely.

Pour the mixture into the bowl of an ice-cream machine. Churn until softly set. Transfer the sorbet to a freezerproof container, cover and freeze overnight until firm.

STRAWBERRY AND HIBISCUS SORBET

If in season, use wild strawberries to make an even more intensely flavoured sorbet.

MAKES ABOUT 1.5 LITRES

240g caster sugar
10g liquid glucose
500ml water
40g dried hibiscus flowers
750g fresh or frozen strawberries
  (thawed if frozen)

Put the sugar, liquid glucose and water into a pan and stir over medium heat until the sugar has dissolved. Add the hibiscus flowers and bring to the boil. Turn the heat down to low, partially cover the pan with a lid and simmer the syrup gently for 10 minutes. Remove from the heat and leave to cool completely, by which time the syrup will have become infused with the flavour of the hibiscus flowers.

Meanwhile, hull the strawberries, if necessary, and cut larger ones into halves or quarters. Put them in a blender. Strain the hibiscus syrup through a fine sieve, then add to the blender. Blitz to a purée. Pass the purée through a fine sieve, pushing the pulp with a spatula, until you are left with just the strawberry seeds in the sieve. Discard the seeds.

Pour the sorbet mixture into the bowl of an ice-cream machine and churn until softly set. Scrape the sorbet into a freezerproof container, then cover and freeze for about 4 hours or overnight until firm.

CHOCOLATE SORBET

MAKES ABOUT 850ML

75g caster sugar
75g liquid glucose
500ml water
200g dark chocolate (with about 70% cocoa solids)

Put the sugar, liquid glucose and water into a heavy-based pan and bring to the boil, stirring until the sugar has dissolved. Leave the sugar syrup to boil for a few minutes. Meanwhile, roughly chop the dark chocolate and place in a heatproof bowl. Pour the hot syrup over the chopped chocolate, stirring until the chocolate has melted and the mixture is smooth.

Leave to cool completely before transferring the mixture to the bowl of an ice-cream machine. Churn until the sorbet is softly set. Scrape the sorbet into a freezerproof container, cover and freeze for at least 4 hours or until firm.

STRAWBERRY SAKE SORBET

MAKES ABOUT 1.3 LITRES

600g strawberries, hulled and roughly
  chopped
190g caster sugar
30g liquid glucose
310ml water
150ml strong sake

Put the strawberries, sugar, liquid glucose and water into a heavy-based saucepan and stir over medium heat for 4–5 minutes or until the sugar and glucose have dissolved and the strawberries are soft but not mushy. Tip the contents of the pan into a blender and blitz to a fine purée. Strain the purée through a fine sieve into a large bowl and leave to cool.

When the mixture is cold, stir in the sake. Pour into the bowl of an ice-cream machine and churn until softly set. Transfer the sorbet to a freezerproof container and freeze overnight or until firm.

PEACH SORBET

MAKES ABOUT 650ML

550g ripe peaches
25g liquid glucose
30g caster sugar
2 tablespoons water

Cut the peaches in half and remove the stones, then roughly chop the flesh. Put the liquid glucose, sugar and water into a saucepan and stir over medium heat until the sugar has dissolved. Increase the heat slightly and bring to a simmer. Add the chopped peaches and poach them in the syrup for 10–15 minutes or until very soft. Take the pan off the heat.

While still hot, tip the contents of the pan into a blender and blitz to a very fine purée. Leave to cool. You can either churn the purée as is or pass it through a fine sieve to remove any bits of skin that have not been blended well.

Pour the mixture into the bowl of an ice-cream machine and churn until softly set. Transfer the sorbet to a freezerproof container, cover and freeze for at least 4 hours or until firm.

PASSION FRUIT SORBET

Passion fruits vary in size and yield so I've listed the amount of strained fresh juice you would need for this recipe. Do not be tempted to use passion fruit juice sold in packs or bottles as drinks because they have added sugar and will affect not only the sweetness but also the setting quality of the sorbet.

MAKES ABOUT 1.5 LITRES

500g caster sugar
50g liquid glucose
500ml water
500ml strained passion fruit juice
(from 20–24 large, ripe passion fruit)

Put the sugar, liquid glucose and water into a saucepan and stir over a medium-high heat until the sugar has dissolved. Add the passion fruit juice, then remove the pan from the heat and pour the mixture into a wide bowl. Leave to cool completely.

Transfer the mixture to the bowl of an ice-cream machine and churn until softly set. Scrape the sorbet into a freezerproof container, cover and freeze for a few hours or until firm.

ICE CREAM & SORBETS

RASPBERRY AND YUZU SORBET

MAKES ABOUT 1.2 LITRES

50g caster sugar
50ml water
50g liquid glucose
1kg fresh or frozen raspberries
   (thawed if frozen)
60ml yuzu (or lime) juice

Put the sugar, water and liquid glucose into a heavy-based saucepan and stir over medium heat until the sugar has dissolved. Increase the heat and bring the sugar syrup to the boil. Tip in the raspberries and take the pan off the heat.

Transfer the mixture to a blender and blitz until smooth. Strain through a fine sieve into a large bowl; discard the raspberry seeds. Stir in the yuzu juice and leave to cool.

Pour the mixture into the bowl of an ice-cream machine and churn until softly set. Scrape the sorbet into a freezerproof container, seal and freeze for at least 4 hours or overnight until firm.

FROMAGE FRAIS (OR YOGHURT) SORBET

MAKES ABOUT 1.7 LITRES

350g caster sugar
100g liquid glucose
350ml water
juice of 2 lemons
800g fromage frais (or full-fat Greek yoghurt)

Combine the sugar, liquid glucose and water in a saucepan and stir over a medium-high heat until the sugar has dissolved. Add the lemon juice, then stir in the fromage frais (or yoghurt). Remove the pan from the heat and strain the mixture through a fine sieve into a wide bowl. (This will help to break up any lumps of fromage frais that remain.) Leave to cool completely.

Churn the mixture in an ice-cream machine until softly set. Scrape the sorbet into a freezerproof container, cover and freeze for at least 4 hours or until firm.

MANGO AND LIME SORBET

209

MAKES ABOUT 1.2 LITRES

1kg mango flesh (from 2–3 large, ripe
  mangoes)
juice of 1–2 limes
75g caster sugar
50g liquid glucose
75ml water

Roughly chop the mango flesh and tip into
a blender. Add the juice of 1 lime.

Put the sugar, liquid glucose and water into
a saucepan and stir over a medium-high
heat until the sugar has dissolved. Pour the
sugar syrup into the blender and blitz until
the mangoes are nicely puréed and the
mixture is smooth. Taste the mixture: if it
is too sweet, add a little more lime juice and
blend again. Strain the mixture through a
fine sieve into a wide bowl, pushing down
on the mango pulp to extract all the juice.
Discard the pulp. Leave to cool completely.

Pour the mango mixture into the bowl
of an ice-cream machine and churn
until softly set. Transfer the sorbet to a
freezerproof container, cover and freeze for
about 4 hours or until firm.

VERBENA AND OLIVE OIL SORBET

To match the fresh, zingy flavours of lemon verbena, use good-quality extra virgin olive oil, preferably one with herby or sweet, fruity aromas.

MAKES ABOUT 1 LITRE

170g caster sugar
200g liquid glucose
200ml water
8g dried lemon verbena leaves
230g fromage frais
40ml lemon juice
125ml extra virgin olive oil

Put the sugar, liquid glucose and water into a saucepan and stir over medium heat until the sugar has dissolved. Increase the heat and bring to the boil. Tip in the lemon verbena leaves and boil the syrup for a couple of minutes. Remove the pan from the heat and leave to cool completely, by which time the syrup will have become infused with the flavour of the lemon verbena.

Strain the syrup and discard the leaves. Whisk the fromage frais, lemon juice and olive oil into the syrup, then pour into the bowl of an ice-cream machine. Churn until the sorbet is softly set. Transfer to a freezerproof container, cover and freeze for several hours or until firm.

ICE CREAM & SORBETS

GREEN BASIL SORBET

MAKES ABOUT 600ML

100g caster sugar
140g liquid glucose
400ml water
80g picked basil leaves
juice of 1 lemon

Put the sugar, liquid glucose and water into a saucepan and stir over a medium-high heat until the sugar has dissolved. Remove from the heat and leave to cool completely. Meanwhile, wash the basil leaves and pat dry with kitchen paper.

Once the syrup has cooled, pour it into a blender and add the basil leaves and lemon juice. Blitz until the basil leaves are finely ground and you have a vivid green syrup. Strain the mixture through a fine sieve into the bowl of an ice-cream machine. Churn until the sorbet is softly set, then transfer to a freezerproof container, cover and freeze until firm.

CHEESE

CHEESE

228/ MANCHEGO, WILD FLOWER HONEY, CHERRIES AND FRESH ALMONDS
229/ GRATINATED PERAIL WITH SALAD OF POTATO, JERUSALEM ARTICHOKE, APPLE AND
PINE NUTS 230/ ROASTED BUTTERNUT SQUASH, SQUASH PURÉE, PARMESAN, TOAST AND
THYME 233/ COMTÉ MOUSSE, PORT REDUCTION AND WILD FLOWERS

CASHEL BLUE, ROASTED ENDIVE AND ROASTED PEAR IN A SPICE SYRUP

Salty blue cheese and sweet pears are a classic pairing, but here I'm taking things to another level by adding roasted endive and a fragrant, spice syrup to the dish. With the sweet spice syrup, the dish can masquerade as either a cheese course or a dessert. Either way, it is truly enjoyable.

SERVES 4

400g Cashel Blue cheese, cut into 4
  neat slices

For the spice syrup
250ml water
90g caster sugar
½ tablespoon lemon juice
2 star anise, lightly crushed
1 cinnamon stick

For the roasted pear
2 ripe pears
20g unsalted butter

For the roasted endive
20g unsalted butter
4 endives (chicory), halved
  lengthways
200ml chicken stock
2 tablespoons lemon juice
sea salt and freshly ground black
  pepper

First prepare the spice syrup. Place all the ingredients in a small saucepan and stir over medium heat until the sugar has dissolved. Increase the heat and bring to the boil, then leave to boil for about 10 minutes or until reduced to a syrupy consistency. Leave to cool completely, then strain the syrup and transfer to a small jar or squeezy bottle, ready for serving.

Trim the tops and bottoms from the pears, then slice horizontally into 1.5cm-thick rounds – you will need four neat slices of fairly equal size and thickness. (The leftover slices and trimmings are a cook's treat.) Melt the butter in a wide frying pan set over medium heat. When the butter begins to foam, add the pear slices and fry for 2–3 minutes on each side or until golden brown. Transfer the pears to a plate lined with kitchen paper to absorb any excess butter.

For the endives, wipe the pan clean with a wad of kitchen paper, then return it to medium-high heat. Add the butter and, as it melts, place the endive halves, cut side down, in the pan. Fry for 2 minutes or until golden brown, then flip the endives over and pour in the stock. Add the lemon juice and a pinch of salt. Lower the heat slightly and simmer gently for about 15 minutes or until the endives are tender but still holding their shape. Remove from the heat and keep the endives warm in the stock.

To serve, place a roasted pear slice in the centre of each serving plate and arrange two well-drained roasted endive halves on either side of the pear. Drizzle the spice syrup over the pear and endive. Place a slice of Cashel Blue on top of the roasted pear. Coarsely grind some black pepper over all and serve immediately.

CHEESE

STILTON, PUFF PASTRY AND BEETROOT

This gorgeous tart tastes as good as it looks but you do need to use good-quality all butter puff pastry. You can make it to serve as a starter or as a cheese course and it is a great way to use up leftover Christmas Stilton.

SERVES 4

200g Quick Puff Pastry (see page 238) or store-bought butter puff pastry
250g Stilton cheese, at room temperature
4 radicchio leaves, cut lengthways into thin strips

For the roasted beetroot
2 large beetroots, about 400g in total
olive oil for drizzling
20g unsalted butter
4 sprigs of rosemary, each cut in half

For the beetroot dressing
1 tablespoon Chardonnay or white wine vinegar
1 tablespoon honey
1 tablespoon caster sugar
1 teaspoon thyme leaves
60ml olive oil
sea salt and freshly ground black pepper

Start with the roasted beetroot. Preheat the oven to 180°C/Fan 160°C/Gas Mark 4. Place the beetroots on a large piece of foil and drizzle over a light coating of oil. Season with a pinch each of salt and pepper, then wrap up in the foil and place on a small roasting tray. Roast the beetroots for 50–60 minutes or until they are tender when pierced with the tip of a small, sharp knife.

Meanwhile, roll out the puff pastry on a lightly floured surface to the thickness of a £1 coin. Cut out four neat rectangles, about 6 x 12cm. Lay them on a baking sheet lined with a silicone mat or baking parchment. Prick the pastry rectangles all over with a fork (this will prevent them from puffing up too much during baking). Cut the Stilton into thin slices and arrange them on top of the puff pastry rectangles. Chill for at least half an hour (or until the beetroot is out of the oven).

Next prepare the beetroot dressing. Put the vinegar, honey and sugar into a screwtop jar, cover and shake to dissolve the sugar. Add the thyme leaves and olive oil and shake well to emulsify. Set aside.

When the roasted beetroot is ready, take it out of the oven and leave to cool slightly before unwrapping. When the beetroots are cool enough to handle, peel off the skins. Cut the beetroots into thin wedges and place them in a large bowl. Spoon over the beetroot dressing and leave to marinate at room temperature for at least 20 minutes.

When you are about ready to serve, melt the butter in a large frying pan over medium heat. Scrape the dressing off the beetroot wedges (save the dressing for later) and add them to the pan along with the rosemary sprigs. Fry for about a minute on each side or until the beetroot wedges are golden brown around the edges. Remove to a plate.

To serve, place a puff pastry rectangle on each serving plate and arrange the beetroot wedges on top. Garnish with the radicchio strips and fried rosemary. Spoon over a little beetroot dressing and serve immediately.

QUARK WITH WHITE CHOCOLATE, MACERATED FIGS, FIG SYRUP AND PAIN D'ÉPICES

This fantastic dish is a way of combining the cheese and dessert courses to delicious effect. Here, soft quark cheese acts as a blank canvas for the sweet macerated figs, white chocolate and spiced gingerbread croutons. For a different presentation, you could make a sweet crostini using the same ingredients. Simply spread the quark onto slices of pain d'epices then top with the macerated figs and white chocolate.

SERVES 4

125g white chocolate, chopped
35g cocoa butter
6 ripe figs
50g icing sugar, sifted
1 teaspoon aged balsamic vinegar
2 slices Pain d'épices (see page 31)
20g unsalted butter
400g quark cheese

Melt the white chocolate with the cocoa butter in a heatproof bowl set on a pan of gently simmering water. As the chocolate softens, stir until the mixture is smooth. Remove the bowl from the pan.

Spread the melted chocolate thinly on a baking sheet lined with a silicone mat or baking parchment. Leave to cool completely. Once the chocolate has cooled and set, break it into small shards and keep in an airtight container until ready to serve.

Cut the figs vertically into quarters and place them in a large bowl. Add the sugar and balsamic vinegar and toss well to coat. Cover the bowl with cling film and leave the figs to macerate in the fridge for about 2 hours. During this time the figs should release some of their juices to create a fig-flavoured syrup with the sugar. (If the juice is not syrupy enough, strain it into a small saucepan and boil for a few minutes until reduced and thickened; cool.)

To make croutons, cut the pain d'épices into 1cm dice. Melt the butter in a frying pan and, as it begins to foam, add the diced bread. Toss to coat with butter, then fry for 2–3 minutes, tossing occasionally, until the croutons are crisp and golden brown. Tip them on to a plate lined with kitchen paper.

To serve, spoon the quark on to four serving plates and arrange the drained macerated figs on top. Scatter the croutons around the plate, then garnish with the white chocolate shards. Drizzle over a little fig syrup and serve immediately.

TRUFFLED BRIE DE MEAUX, APPLE RAVIOLI AND CELERY LEAVES

If you happen to win the lottery, you should definitely make this truffled brie. Buy the best truffle on the market and use it to transform a brie de meaux into the most amazing cheese. However, if you are on a shoestring budget and can't afford to put a fresh truffle on your shopping list, get a small bottle of truffle oil and drizzle the brie with it. You would only need a few drops so save the truffle oil to use in other dishes. The apple ravioli is lovely and refreshing but if you are short of time, just serve the truffled brie with fresh apple slices and celery leaves.

SERVES 4

For the truffled brie
2 tablespoons mascarpone
1 Brie de Meaux, weighing 250–300g
2 tablespoons black Périgord truffle paste
1 fresh black Périgord truffle
black truffle oil, for drizzling
sea salt

For the apple ravioli
½ lemon, for squeezing
3 Granny Smith apples
20g unsalted butter
1–2 tablespoons icing sugar (optional)

To serve
a handful of young celery leaves

In a small bowl, mix the mascarpone with a pinch of sea salt and stir well. Cut the cheese in half horizontally, then spread a thin layer of mascarpone on the cut sides of each half. Place the brie halves, cut side up, on a plate and leave in the fridge to firm up for 20–30 minutes, uncovered.

Spread a thin layer of truffle paste on top of a brie half. Shave black truffle (as much as you like) evenly over the top of the other brie half, making sure not to leave any area uncovered. Drizzle a little black truffle oil over the shaved black truffle, then sandwich the halves together to reform the cheese. Wrap the brie in cling film and press down gently. Chill for at least an hour or until the cheese is firm.

Next prepare the apple ravioli. Have ready a bowl of cold water with a squeeze of lemon juice added. Peel the apples. Cut one in half and put half into the acidulated water with another whole apple; set aside. Remove the core from the other half and remaining whole peeled apple, then roughly chop the flesh. Put this into a small saucepan with the butter and a little splash of water and cook over medium heat, stirring frequently, for 10–12 minutes or until very soft. Transfer to a food processor and blitz until smooth. Pass this apple purée through a fine sieve into a bowl. Taste and add a little icing sugar if you find it too tart. Leave to cool.

Very finely slice the remaining whole peeled apple into thin rounds using a mandoline (you will need eight large rounds). Immediately return the rounds to the bowl of acidulated water.

When the apple purée has cooled, core the remaining half peeled apple and cut into a fine 3–4mm dice. Fold into the purée. Cover and keep in the fridge until needed.

Half an hour before you are ready to serve, unwrap the cold brie and cut it into four portions. Place a portion on each serving plate and set aside to allow the cheese to come to room temperature.

Assemble the apple ravioli just before serving. Drain the apple rounds and pat dry with kitchen paper, then lay them out on a flat surface. Spoon a dollop of the apple purée on the middle of each one. Fold over the apple slices into a half-moon shapes. Add two apple raviolis to each serving plate, garnish with celery leaves and serve immediately.

BAKED VACHERIN, NEW POTATOES, TOAST AND CORNICHONS

A couple of years ago, I took my girls on a ski trip to the Swiss Alps. One afternoon, I decided to venture off on my own and I stumbled upon a tiny restaurant serving raclette. Although I was familiar with the dish, it was the first time I had ordered it for myself. It was a revelation to discover that something as simple as melted cheese, potatoes, bread and cornichons could be so delicious. I could happily devour this on my own, but it is better enjoyed as a dish to share amongst family or friends.

SERVES 4

1 whole vacherin Mont d'Or, weighing
   350–450g
a sprig of rosemary, cut into 5 pieces
3 sprigs of thyme
2 garlic cloves, peeled and thinly
   sliced
150ml dry white wine

For the fried new potatoes
16 similar-sized new potatoes,
   800–900g in total
1 litre chicken stock
30g unsalted butter
3 tablespoons olive oil
sea salt

To serve
16 slices of baguette
24 cornichons

First prepare the new potatoes. Put them (unpeeled) into a medium-sized pan and add the stock and add a generous pinch of sea salt. If the stock does not cover the potatoes, top up with a little water. Set the pan over medium heat and bring to a simmer. Cook for 10–15 minutes or until the potatoes are just cooked through (when you pierce the thickest part of a potato with the tip of a knife, there should be little resistance). Remove from the heat and leave the potatoes to cool in the stock.

Once the potatoes have cooled, drain them (you can reserve the stock to cook pasta or for another use) and cut them in half lengthways. Heat the butter with 2 tablespoons of the oil in a large frying pan over medium-high heat, then add the potato halves and fry for about 2 minutes on each side or until golden brown. Using a slotted spoon, remove the potatoes to a tray lined with kitchen paper to absorb excess fat. Set aside in a warm place.

Return the frying pan (with the fat left in it) to the heat. Add the remaining tablespoon of oil and fry the slices of baguette for 1–2 minutes on each side or until they are crisp and golden brown around the edges. (You may need to do this in two batches if your pan is not large enough to accommodate the slices in one layer.) Remove them to a plate and set aside.

Preheat the oven to 180°C/Fan 160°C/Gas Mark 4. Remove all the packaging from the vacherin and place it in a deep ovenproof dish. Make slits in the cheese with the tip of a small knife, then stud it with the rosemary, thyme and garlic slices. Pour over the wine. Bake for 10–12 minutes or until the cheese is meltingly soft.

Remove from the oven and allow to cool for a couple of minutes, during which time you can put the potatoes into the still-hot oven to reheat. Serve the vacherin with the toasts, fried new potatoes and cornichons on the side.

CHEESE

SOCIAL SWEETS

LINCOLNSHIRE POACHER, CAULIFLOWER FONDUE

This dish is an adaptation of a vegetarian starter we served at Social Eating House. We came up with it as a way to create a fondue-like consistency using leftover mash and melted cheese. Lincolnshire poacher is an unpasteurised cow's milk cheese with a slightly similar taste profile to West Country cheddar. If you can't source it, substitute with any good mature cheddar.

SERVES 4

For the Lincolnshire Poacher pomme purée
150g La Ratte or Anya potatoes
60g unsalted butter
2 tablespoons double cream
1 tablespoon whole milk
350g Lincolnshire Poacher cheese (or equal quantities of Gruyère and mild Cheddar), grated
sea salt

For the pan-roasted cauliflower
1 tablespoon olive oil
30g unsalted butter
12 purple cauliflower florets, about 60g in total
12 white cauliflower florets, about 60g in total

To serve
4–5 slices of jamón ibérico (or Parma ham), at room temperature, torn into bite-sized pieces
1 radicchio castelfranco, torn into bite-sized pieces

First prepare the pomme purée. Put the potatoes (unpeeled) into a pan of water and add a generous pinch of salt. Bring to the boil, then lower the heat slightly and simmer for 20 minutes or until the potatoes are tender when pierced with the tip of a knife. Drain well and leave to cool for a few minutes.

While still hot (wear rubber gloves to protect your hands), peel off the skins with the help of a small knife. Finely mash the potatoes using a potato ricer (or push the potatoes through a fine sieve). Next heat the butter, cream and milk in a pan until the butter has melted. Add the mashed potatoes and stir well to mix. Set aside.

To cook the cauliflower, heat the oil and butter in a wide pan. Once the butter begins to foam, tip in the cauliflower florets and add a pinch of salt. Toss the cauliflower to coat with the butter, then fry for 3–4 minutes or until the florets are evenly golden brown. Using a slotted spoon, remove the cauliflower to a plate lined with kitchen paper to absorb the excess fat. Reserve the browned butter in the pan for drizzling later.

Reheat the pomme purée over medium heat, then add 250g of the grated cheese and stir well to mix. Once the cheese has melted and the mixture is quite smooth, take the pan off the heat.

Divide the cheesey pomme purée among four warmed plates. Top with cauliflower florets, ham and radicchio. Drizzle a little of the reserved browned butter over each serving and sprinkle with the remaining grated cheese. Serve at once.

MANCHEGO, WILD FLOWER HONEY, CHERRIES AND FRESH ALMONDS

Cherries and almonds come into season at the same time over a short period in early summer and I love putting the two fresh ingredients together to make this cheese plate. Together with the wild flower honey and thyme, the cherries and almonds make the perfect accompaniment to wonderful Manchego cheese. Fresh young almonds have a mildly nutty flavour and soft texture, not dissimilar to Kentish cobnuts. If they are out of season (or difficult to source), substitute with toasted flaked almonds or roasted Marcona almonds.

SERVES 4

400g manchego cheese
20 fresh green almonds
40 fresh cherries (about 270g in
    total)
2 sprigs of lemon thyme, leaves
    picked

For the simple dressing
4 tablespoons white wine or sherry
    vinegar
140ml extra virgin olive oil
sea salt and freshly ground black
    pepper
4 teaspoons wild flower honey

Remove the manchego from the fridge and let it come to room temperature while you prepare the rest of the dish.

Cut each almond in half, then pick out the nut. Roughly chop the nuts and put them in a bowl. Remove the stones from the cherries, then cut each fruit into quarters. Add to the bowl along with the thyme leaves.

In a separate small bowl, stir together the vinegar and oil with seasoning to taste to make the dressing. Add the honey and mix well. Spoon the dressing over the almonds and cherries and toss well to coat. Set aside for 15–20 minutes to allow the flavours to mingle.

To serve, cut the cheese into four equal portions and place a piece on each serving plate. Spoon the cherry and almond mixture over the cheese and drizzle any remaining dressing around the plates. Serve as is or with some toasted country bread on the side.

GRATINATED PERAIL WITH SALAD OF POTATO, JERUSALEM ARTICHOKE, APPLE AND PINE NUTS

Perail de Brebis is a soft, creamy and full-flavoured cheese made from unpasteurised ewe's milk in the Midi-Pyrénées region of France, traditionally as a secondary product by Roquefort cheesemakers. You can find it at good cheesemongers, but if it proves elusive, substitute with another soft-ripened sheep's milk cheese.

SERVES 4

4 boiled new potatoes
a squeeze of lemon juice
4 Jerusalem artichokes
1 Pink Lady apple
1 quantity Simple Dressing (see
    Manchego, Wild Flower Honey,
    Cherries and Fresh Almonds page
    228)
8 sprigs of thyme, leaves picked
100g toasted pine nuts
4 slices of brown sourdough
1 disc of perail cheese, about 100g

Peel the boiled potatoes, then cut them into 1cm dice. Put into a large mixing bowl.

Have ready a large bowl of cold water with a squeeze of lemon juice added. Peel the Jerusalem artichokes and cut into 1cm dice. As you chop each one, immediately place in the bowl of acidulated water to prevent the dice from turning brown. Do the same for the apple: peel and core it, then cut into 1cm dice and add to the bowl of water.

In a small bowl, mix the dressing with the thyme leaves and toasted pine nuts. Drain the water from the apples and artichokes, then add them to the bowl containing the potatoes. Add the dressing and toss well to coat.

Preheat the grill to the highest setting. Lay the sourdough slices on a baking sheet and lightly toast on both sides under the grill. Slice the cheese and arrange the slices evenly over the sourdough toasts. Grill for 2–4 minutes, watching closely as the cheese can easily burn, until the cheese has melted and is light golden brown.

Place a cheese toast on each individual serving plate and top with the potato, apple and artichoke mixture. Serve at once.

ROASTED BUTTERNUT SQUASH, SQUASH PURÉE, PARMESAN, TOAST AND THYME

These squash and Parmesan crostini make great little snacks to enjoy with drinks or to follow a main course as a lovely alternative to a cheese platter. If possible, use a good aged Parmesan to make all the difference to the dish.

SERVES 4

1 butternut squash (or small
    pumpkin), weighing 900g–1kg
100g unsalted butter
12 sprigs of thyme
12 slices of baguette
250g Parmesan cheese (150g grated
    and 100g shaved)
Vanilla Stock Syrup (see page 242), for
    drizzling
sea salt and freshly ground black
    pepper

Cut the butternut squash in half lengthways and scoop out the seeds and fibres with a spoon. Cut the halves across to separate the bulbous top from the bottom part. Slice the bulbous parts into thin wedges, each about 1–1.5cm thick. You need 12 neat wedges. Set these aside. Peel the remaining squash (including any extra wedges) and roughly chop the flesh.

Melt 75g of the butter in a large frying pan over medium heat. Add the chopped squash and stir to coat with the melted butter, then cook, stirring occasionally, for about 15 minutes or until very soft (the squash should not brown). Tip the hot squash into a food processor and blitz until smooth. Season with salt and pepper to taste. Pour into a pan. If you find the purée too watery, simmer until it has thickened slightly. Set aside (in the pan).

Melt the remaining butter in a large frying pan over medium-high heat. When it begins to foam, add the squash wedges and season with a little salt and pepper. Fry for 4–5 minutes, turning occasionally, until the squash is golden brown and tender. Add the thyme sprigs during the last minute. Using a slotted spoon, remove the squash and thyme from the pan to a plate lined with kitchen paper. Keep warm in a low oven.

Add the baguette slices to the butter remaining in the pan and fry for 1–2 minutes on each side or until evenly golden brown. Remove to a plate (keep the browned butter in the pan) and place in the low oven to keep warm.

Reheat the squash purée over medium heat. Add the grated Parmesan and mix well until the cheese has melted and the purée is smooth again.

To serve, put three pieces of toast on each warmed serving plate. Place a wedge of fried squash on each toast and add a generous spoonful of Parmesan and squash purée. Garnish with the fried thyme sprigs and Parmesan shavings. Finally, drizzle a little vanilla stock syrup and any remaining browned butter from the pan over the plates. Serve at once.

CHEESE

SOCIAL SWEETS

COMTÉ MOUSSE, PORT REDUCTION AND WILD FLOWERS

I adore Comté cheese and in this dish I have transformed it into a lovely set mousse to serve with an intense port reduction. The cheese mousse will set hard in the fridge so do make sure to give it plenty of time to soften at room temperature. Enjoy with a glass of port or spicy red wine.

SERVES 4

375ml port
1 leaf of gelatine
500g aged Comté cheese, roughly
    chopped or grated
4 tablespoons whole milk
2 tablespoons double cream
flavourless vegetable oil for greasing
    the ramekins
a large handful of edible flowers and
    mixed herbs, to garnish

First, make the port reduction. Pour the port into a saucepan and bring to the boil. Let it boil for 5–10 minutes or until it has reduced to a syrupy consistency. Take care not to over-reduce the port or it will become bitter. Leave to cool completely, then pour into a small jar or squeezy bottle, ready for serving.

Soak the gelatine sheet in a bowl of cold water. Put the cheese into a small pan, add the milk and cream, and place the pan over medium heat. Stir constantly until the cheese has melted and the mixture is smooth. Squeeze out the excess water from the gelatine, then add to the pan and stir until the gelatine has melted. Divide the cheese mixture among four lightly oiled ramekins. Leave to cool, then place in the fridge to set.

About 30 minutes before serving, remove the ramekins from the fridge and run a small knife around the inside of each to loosen the cheese mousse. Turn out on to individual serving plates. Leave for at least 30 minutes to let the cheese come to room temperature. Garnish each plate with wild flowers and herbs, then drizzle over the port reduction. Serve as is or with some thin slices of toast on the side.

basics

Basics

QUICK PUFF PASTRY

238

MAKES ABOUT 625G

For the détrempe (base dough)
165g plain flour
1 teaspoon fine sea salt
25g unsalted butter, diced
4–6 tablespoons cold water
1 medium egg yolk
1½ teaspoons white wine vinegar

For the layering butter
85g plain flour
225g unsalted butter, cold but pliable

First, make the détrempe. Sift the flour and salt into the bowl of an electric mixer fitted with the paddle attachment. Add the diced butter and mix on low speed until the mixture is crumbly. Make a well in the centre.

Put 4 tablespoons of the water into a small bowl, add the egg yolk and vinegar, and lightly beat together with a fork. Pour this mixture into the well. Mix on low speed until the dough starts to come together. If it seems too dry, add a little more water a tablespoon at a time (try not to add too much water or the resulting pastry will be tough). Roughly shape the dough into a rectangular block, measuring about 15 x 20cm, then wrap in cling film and leave in the fridge to relax for half an hour.

Next, prepare the layering butter. Put the flour and butter into the mixer bowl and mix on low speed until just combined. Scrape the mixture on to a large piece of cling film. Using the cling film to help, shape the mixture into a rough rectangle, slightly smaller than the détrempe. Wrap well and refrigerate for an hour.

Remove both the détrempe and the layering butter from the fridge. (If the layering butter is very hard, let it soften for a few minutes at room temperature; return the détrempe to the fridge in the meantime.) Unwrap the détrempe and place it on a floured work surface so that a short side is closest to you. Gently roll it out away from you until it is about twice the original length – to about 20 x 40cm. As you are rolling out the dough, try to keep edges straight and even.

Unwrap the layering butter and place it on the bottom half of the détrempe (the end closest to you), centring it so there is a 1cm border around three sides. Fold up the three borders around the butter, then fold down the top half of the détrempe to cover the butter. Lightly press the edges with the rolling pin to seal in the butter layer.

Now gently roll out the dough again until it is three times as long as it is wide, trying as much as possible to keep the edges straight. Fold up the bottom third of the dough over the middle third, then fold down the top third over the middle (as if you were folding a business letter). Give the dough a quarter turn clockwise, then roll it out to three times the length, as before. Once again, fold the bottom third up over the middle and then the top third down. Wrap the dough in cling film and refrigerate for half an hour.

Roll out and fold the dough four more times, giving it a 30-minute rest in the fridge halfway through (i.e. after the next two rolls and folds). If during the rolling out and folding, the butter layer breaks through the détrempe, sprinkle it with flour and dust off any excess with a dry pastry brush. The pastry should be cold to the touch throughout the rolling and folding; if it gets too warm, it will become greasy and heavy. So if necessary, return the dough to the fridge and chill for 30 minutes before continuing.

Once the dough has had a total of six rolls and folds, wrap it well in cling film and keep in the fridge until ready to use.

SWEET PASTRY

CHOUX PASTRY

CHOCOLATE SWEET PASTRY

MAKES ABOUT 550G

100g unsalted butter, softened
50g icing sugar, sifted
50g caster sugar
250g plain flour
1 large egg, lightly beaten

Put the softened butter and both sugars into a large mixing bowl and beat with a wooden spoon until smooth and creamy. (If you want to double or triple the recipe, you can cream the butter and sugars together using an electric whisk; however, do not overbeat the mixture until it is fluffy, as you don't want to incorporate too much air.) Add the flour and egg alternately, in two batches each, and mix until just combined.

Gather the dough together and lightly knead it on a lightly floured surface. Wrap in cling film and refrigerate for at least 30 minutes before rolling out. (Any excess pastry can be wrapped and frozen for up to a month.)

MAKES ABOUT 750G (ENOUGH TO MAKE ABOUT 30 ÉCLAIRS)

250ml water
110g unsalted butter
5g fine sea salt
140g plain flour
4 medium eggs, lightly beaten

Put the water, butter and salt into a pan and warm over medium heat until the butter has melted. Increase the heat to high and let the liquid come to a rolling boil. Meanwhile, sift the flour twice on to a sheet of baking parchment. When the liquid in the pan is boiling, pick up the edges of the parchment and tip all the flour into the pan in one go. Quickly use a wooden spoon to beat the mixture vigorously for 20–30 seconds or until it comes together and pulls away from the sides of the pan.

Transfer the dough to the bowl of an electric mixer fitted with the paddle attachment. On low speed, beat in the eggs a little at a time. You may not need all the egg – add just enough to achieve a shiny, glossy dough with a dropping consistency (the dough should fall off a spoon in about 5 seconds). Let the pastry cool before using.

MAKES ABOUT 650G

275g plain flour
20g cocoa powder
½ teaspoon fine sea salt
40g ground almonds
160g unsalted butter, softened
115g icing sugar, sifted
1 large egg, lightly beaten

Sift the flour, cocoa powder and salt into a mixing bowl, then stir in the ground almonds. In another mixing bowl, beat together the softened butter and icing sugar. Gradually beat in the egg, then add the flour mixture and mix well until just combined.

Press the mixture into a ball of dough and lightly knead on a lightly floured surface. (Try not to overwork the dough or the resulting pastry will be tough.) Wrap in cling film and refrigerate for at least 30 minutes before using. The pastry freezes well and can be kept for up to a month.

CRÈME PÂTISSIÈRE (PASTRY CREAM)

VANILLA CRÈME ANGLAISE

CRÈME CHANTILLY

MAKES ABOUT 550ML

500ml whole milk
1 vanilla pod, split in half, seeds
    scraped out with a knife
4 large egg yolks
150g caster sugar
50g cornflour

Put the milk and vanilla seeds and pod into a small saucepan and bring to the boil. Meanwhile, beat the egg yolks and sugar together in a bowl, then mix in the cornflour until smooth. As soon as the creamy milk comes up to the boil, slowly pour it into the yolk mixture, whisking constantly. Fish out the vanilla pod, then strain the mixture through a fine sieve into a clean pan.

Set the pan over high heat and let the mixture come to the boil. Cook for 3–4 minutes or until the crème pâtissière is smooth and thick (and does not have a floury aftertaste). Pour into a bowl and lay a piece of cling film on the surface to prevent a skin from forming. Leave to cool completely before using. The crème pâtissière can be kept in the fridge for up to 3 days.

MAKES ABOUT 300ML

250ml double cream
½ vanilla pod, split in half, seeds
    scraped out with a knife
65g caster sugar
3 large egg yolks

Heat the cream with the vanilla seeds and pod in a saucepan until it begins to boil. Remove from the heat and let the vanilla infuse the cream as it cools.

Meanwhile, beat the sugar and egg yolks together in a large bowl. When the vanilla cream has cooled, fish out the pod, then mix the cream with the sugary yolks. Pour the mixture through a fine sieve into a clean saucepan. Set over a low heat and cook, stirring constantly with a wooden spoon, until the mixture thickens into a thin custard that will lightly coat the back of the spoon.

To make sure the custard is very smooth, pass it through a fine sieve again into a bowl. If not using immediately, cool it down quickly by sitting the bowl in a larger bowl of iced water; stir occasionally to prevent a skin from forming. Keep in the fridge and use within a few days.

MAKES ABOUT 275G

250ml double cream
25g icing sugar, sifted
½ vanilla pod, split open, seeds
    scraped out with a knife

Put the cream, sugar and vanilla seeds into a large mixing bowl and whip for a few minutes until soft peaks will form. Cover the bowl with cling film and keep in the fridge until needed (best if used the same day).

SERVES 4

12–16 small picked herb leaves (such
   as mint, tarragon or basil)
1 egg white, lightly beaten
3–4 tablespoons caster sugar

Wash the herb leaves and pat dry with
kitchen paper. Brush each leaf with egg
white so that the whole leaf is covered,
then dip in the sugar to coat and place on
a plate. Leave the leaves to dry for a few
hours before storing in an airtight container.

MAKES ABOUT 75G

3 mandarin oranges
100g caster sugar
200ml water

Bring three small saucepans of water
to the boil. Peel the skins from the
mandarin oranges (reserve the flesh for
eating) and use a small, sharp knife to
trim off any white pith. Cut the peel into
long, thin strips.

Drop the mandarin strips into one of
the pans of boiling water and blanch
for a minute. Drain in a fine sieve and
refresh under cold running water to cool
the peel quickly. Drop it into the second
pan of boiling water and repeat the
blanching and refreshing. Do this one
more time with the third pan of boiling
water. The repeated blanching will help
to remove bitterness from the peel.

In a small saucepan, dissolve the sugar
in the measured water over medium
heat. When the sugar syrup starts to
simmer, add the blanched mandarin
peel and poach for about 10 minutes or
until tender. Take the pan off the heat
and leave to cool.

Transfer the peel and syrup to a small
jar, seal and keep in the fridge until
needed. The candied peel can be kept
for a few weeks.

SERVES 10–12

1 small (or ½ large) ripe pineapple

Preheat the oven to 100°C/Fan 80°C/Gas
Mark ¼. Cut off the skin from around the
pineapple, then lay it on its side and cut
across into four pieces. Turn each piece
upright, so it is on one of the flat sides, and
use a small metal pastry cutter to stamp
out the central core. Carefully slice each
quarter into thin rings (1–2mm or as thin
as possible).

Arrange the pineapple rings on two baking
sheets lined with silicone mats. Place in
the oven and leave to dry out for about 1
hour, gently turning the slices over halfway
through. During the last 15 minutes of
baking, keep an eye on the rings as they can
burn easily. They are ready when they are
light golden brown and crisp. Remove, cool
and store in an airtight container.

MAKES ABOUT 750ML

500g caster sugar
500ml water
a squeeze of lemon juice (optional)

Stir the sugar and water in a saucepan over low heat to dissolve the sugar. Increase the heat and bring to the boil. Boil for a few minutes until the syrup thickens slightly, then remove from the heat and leave to cool completely. Once cooled, stir in the lemon juice. If not using immediately, pour the syrup into a clean container or squeezy bottle and keep in the fridge for up to 2 weeks.

Variation
For Vanilla Stock Syrup, omit the lemon juice and add the seeds from a vanilla pod plus the empty pod to the hot syrup. Fish out the pod once the syrup has cooled.

MAKES ABOUT 220G

65g ground almonds
65g caster sugar
35g plain flour
25g cocoa powder
½ teaspoon fine sea salt
30g unsalted butter, melted

Preheat the oven to 150°C/Fan 130°C/Gas Mark 2. Combine all the dry ingredients in a mixing bowl. Add the melted butter and stir until well combined and the mixture resembles fine crumbs.

Spread out the mixture on a baking sheet and bake for about 10 minutes or until dry and crisp. Leave to cool completely before storing in an airtight container (the chocolate soil can be kept for several weeks).

LEMON CURD

RASPBERRY CURD

MAKES ABOUT 490G

3 large eggs
75g caster sugar
75ml lemon juice (from about 3 large
   lemons)
125g cold unsalted butter, diced

Put the eggs, sugar and lemon juice into
a heatproof mixing bowl and give the
mixture a stir. Set the bowl over a pan of
gently simmering water (the base of the
bowl should not touch the water) and whisk
the mixture for 5–8 minutes or until it
thickens to a custard-like consistency. (It is
important to keep stirring or whisking the
mixture over gentle heat or you may end
up with scrambled eggs.)

As soon as the mixture has thickened,
remove the bowl from the pan and slowly
whisk in the butter, a few knobs at a time.
If you want a really smooth finish, pass the
lemon curd through a fine sieve. Let the
curd cool completely, giving it a stir every
now and then to stop a skin from forming;
the curd will thicken further as it cools.
Transfer to a sterilised jar. Keep in the
fridge and use within 3–4 days.

Variations
* To make a thicker and more stable lemon
curd, add ⅔ teaspoon of agar agar powder
to the egg, sugar and lemon juice mixture
before you start to cook it.
* You can make a lime curd by replacing
the lemon juice with lime juice.

MAKES 350G

200g fresh or frozen raspberries
   (thawed if frozen)
50g caster sugar
2 medium eggs
45g cold unsalted butter, diced

Put the raspberries in a bowl and purée
roughly using a stick blender (or mash them
using a potato masher). Pass through a fine
sieve into a large heatproof bowl, pushing
down on the pulp with the back of a ladle
to extract as much juice as possible. Add
the sugar and eggs to the bowl.

Set the bowl over a saucepan of gently
simmering water (make sure that the water
does not touch the base of the bowl). Whisk
the mixture until the sugar has dissolved,
then keep whisking for 5–8 minutes or until
the mixture has visibly thickened. Take the
bowl off the pan and whisk in the butter, a
few pieces at a time.

Transfer the curd to a clean sterilised jar,
cover and leave to cool. Chill for at least 8
hours or until set. The curd can be kept in
the fridge for 1–2 weeks, or frozen for up
to a year.

RASPBERRY JAM

DAMSON JAM

CHERRY JAM

MAKES ABOUT 500G

500g fresh or frozen raspberries
100g caster sugar
10g powdered pectin

Place a small plate or saucer into the freezer to chill (unless you are going to use a sugar thermometer to test the jam). Put the raspberries into a heavy-based pan and set over high heat. Stir the sugar and pectin together, then add to the pan. Stir well. Bring the mixture to the boil. Put in a sugar thermometer, if using. Boil for about 5 minutes or until the jam reaches 107°C. To test if the jam is ready without a thermometer, reduce the heat under the pan and drop a small spoonful of jam on to the chilled plate. Push your finger through the jam: if it is ready, it will wrinkle. If it doesn't wrinkle, boil the jam for a further 2 minutes, then test again.

Once ready, transfer the jam to sterilised jars. Leave to cool completely before sealing. The jam can be kept for about a year, but once opened store in the fridge and consume within a week.

MAKES ABOUT 500G

500g damsons, washed
150ml water
500g preserving sugar
juice of 1 lemon

If you are not using a sugar thermometer to test the jam, place a small plate or saucer into the freezer to chill. Halve the damsons and remove the stones, then cut the fruit into quarters. Put the damsons into a heavy-based saucepan and add the water. Set the saucepan on low heat and give the mixture a stir, then cook gently, stirring every once in a while, for 20–30 minutes or until the damsons are soft and the water has reduced by half. Add the sugar and stir until it has dissolved.

Turn up the heat and bring the mixture to the boil. Put in a sugar thermometer, if using. Boil for 10–12 minutes or until the jam reaches 107°C; stir frequently while the jam is boiling to prevent it from catching on the base of the pan. If you aren't using a sugar thermometer, reduce the heat under the pan and drop a small teaspoonful of jam on to the chilled plate. Return it to the fridge for a couple of minutes, then push the jam with your finger: if it is ready, it will wrinkle. If it doesn't wrinkle, boil the jam for a few more minutes and test again.

Add the lemon juice to the jam and mix well, then leave it to settle for a few minutes. While the jam is still hot, spoon it into warm, sterilised jars and seal well. The jam keeps well for about a year; once opened, store it in the fridge and eat within a week or two.

MAKES ABOUT 460G

500g cherries
7g powdered pectin
juice of ½ lemon
75g caster sugar

Place a small plate or saucer into the freezer to chill (unless you are going to use a sugar thermometer to test the jam). Stone the cherries and roughly chop them. Place them in a heavy-based saucepan and add just enough water to cover. Simmer the cherries for 10–15 minutes, stirring every once in a while, until they are soft. Tip the hot mixture into a food processor and blitz until smooth.

Pour the cherry purée back into the pan and add the rest of the ingredients. Bring to the boil. Put in a sugar thermometer, if using, and boil for 10–12 minutes, stirring frequently to prevent the jam from catching and burning, until it reaches 107°C. To test if the jam is ready without a thermometer, reduce the heat under the pan and drop a small spoonful of jam on to the chilled plate. Push your finger through the jam: if it is ready, it will wrinkle. If it doesn't wrinkle, boil the jam for a further 2 minutes, then test again.

While the jam is still hot, spoon it into warm, sterilised jars and seal well. It can be stored in a cool, dry place for about a year. Once opened, keep in the fridge and consume within a week or two.

INDEX

INDEX

INDEX

ACKNOWLEDGEMENTS

I would like to thank my publisher Jon Croft for his constant support and belief in my abilities and for allowing me this opportunity to create my first ever dessert book, of which I am extremely proud. My sincere thanks to Meg Avent for her endless patience and her guidance with this book. To Matt Inwood and Kim Musgrove for their creative eye and direction and for producing such a beautiful looking book. To Alice Gibbs for getting this project off the ground and to Emily Holmes for somehow managing to get me to deliver everything to her schedule and for keeping it fun all the way through.

A huge thank you to Emily Quah for staying up into the early hours to test recipes and ingredients and for coordinating everything so smoothly – Emily you are a star! To Norma MacMillan and Zoë Ross for their attention to detail, ensuring all the text in this book is as beautiful as the dishes. My thanks to Jo Harris for organising all the prop styling and for managing to set things just as I like them, which is not easy as I'm incredibly fussy!

To John Carey, my very talented and loyal friend, for all the photography in this book and for making my dishes look as beautiful as they taste – there is no one else who quite captures my dishes and what I do like you. Thank you for all your support through the years, John.

A huge thank you to my executive team. To my wife Irha for keeping the business running smoothly and whose constant support is invaluable to me. To Anne-Marie Kinane who coordinated me and the team to ensure everything was always organised for this book. To Michael West, Laure Patry, Gareth Evens, Scott Ashby and Sarah Hutchins for keeping all other aspects of the business afloat while I was away.

To my right-hand man and chef Cary Docherty at Little Social who worked endlessly behind the scenes ensuring everything ran smoothly and seamlessly and without whom this book would not be here today. Cary, you are a massive support and talent.

A huge thank you to my chefs at all my London restaurants for their constant support – Paul Hood at Social Eating House, Phil Carmichael at Berners Tavern, Paul Walsh at City Social, Lee Westcott at Typing Room. To my team of chefs at Pollen Street Social – Ross Bryans, Dale Bainbridge and Alex Craciun – who kept the restaurant running smoothly while I was often away for days out of the kitchen working on this book.

To all my chefs abroad. In Singapore, to Colin Buchan at Pollen and to Andrew Walsh at Esquina and The Study. In Hong Kong, to Chris Whitmore at Aberdeen Street Social and Nathan Green of 22 Ships and Ham & Sherry. In Shanghai, to Scott Melvin at Table 1 and to Christopher Pitts at The Commune Social. Team – thank you for your endless support.

Jason

Publisher Jon Croft
Commissioning Editor Meg Avent
Art Direction Kim Musgrove and Matt Inwood
Design Kim Musgrove
Project Editor Alice Gibbs and Emily Holmes
Editor Norma MacMillan
Photographer John Carey
Home Economy Emily Quah
Props Stylist Jo Harris
Indexer Zoe Ross

A note about the text
This book was set using Baskerville, a serif typeface designed in 1757 by John Baskerville (1706–1775) in Birmingham, England. It is classified as a 'transitional' typeface, in appearance bridging the gap between the old-style faces of William Caslon and the modern styles of Giambattista Bodoni and Firmin Didot.